jump

WHAT LIES DO I BELIEVE?

believe

THE VOICES OF OTHER LOVES

soar

WHISPERS OF UNBELIEF

dance

TIME TO DANCE!

WildAboutYou

AUTHOR
ANGELA THOMAS
Do You Think I'm Beautiful?
The inspiration for *Wild About You*

EDITORIAL
PAM GIBBS Editor In Chief
IVEY HARRINGTON BECKMAN Editor
KRISTI CHERRY Copy Editor
JENNIFER WILSON Teen Editorial Consultant

DESIGN & PRODUCTION
EDWARD CRAWFORD Art Director
JUDY HEWITT Lead Technical Specialist

departments

WILD ABOUT YOU (ISBN: 1-4158-2602-1) Dewey Decimal Classification Number: 248.83 Subject Heading: GIRLS\TEENAGERS\PROVIDENCE AND GOVERNMENT OF GOD. Published by LifeWay Press® Copyright © 2006 by Angela Thomas. Reprinted 2006, January 2007. No part of this work may be reproduced or transmitted in any form or by any means, electronic or mechanical, including photocopying and recording, or by any information storage or retrieval system, except as may be expressly permitted in writing by the publisher. Requests for permission should be addressed in writing to LifeWay Press®, Student Ministry Publishing, One LifeWay Plaza, Nashville, TN 37234-0174. Printed in the United States of America.

We believe the Bible has God for its author; salvation for its end; and truth, without any mixture of error, for its matter and that all Scripture is totally true and trustworthy. The 2000 statement of *The Baptist Faith and Message* is our doctrinal guideline.

Unless otherwise indicated, all Scripture quotations are taken from the *Holman Christian Standard Bible®* Copyright © 1999, 2000, 2002, 2003 by Holman Bible Publishers. Used by permission. *Holman Christian Standard Bible®*, Holman CSB®, and HCSB® are federally registered trademarks of Holman Bible Publishers. Scripture quotations marked (NIV) are taken from the *Holy Bible, New International Version*, copyright © 1973, 1978, 1984 by International Bible Society. Scripture quotations marked (NLT) are taken from the *Holy Bible, New Living Translation*, copyright © 1996. Used by permission of Tyndale House Publishers, Inc., Wheaton, IL 60189 USA. All rights reserved. Scripture quotations marked *(THE MESSAGE)* are taken from *THE MESSAGE*. Copyright © by Eugene H. Peterson, 1993, 1994, 1995. Used by permission of NavPress Publishing Group. Scripture quotations marked (NCV) are taken from *The Holy Bible, New Century Version*, copyright © 1987, 1988, 1991 by W Publishing Group, Nashville, TN 37214. Used by permission.

Published in association with Creative Trust, Inc., 2105 Elliston Place, Nashville, TN 37203. For more information about Angela Thomas, e-mail info@creativetrust.com or visit *www.angelathomas.com*.

Derived from the book *Do You Think I'm Beautiful?*, copyright © 2003 by Angela Thomas and published with the agreement of Thomas Nelson Publishers.

ON THE COVER

Sarah Clark is a high school senior in Paducah, Kentucky. Knowing that God is wild about her makes her feel good and reminds her that others' opinions of her don't really matter. Sarah's message to you is that character is what counts and how you treat others is more important than how you look!

Cover Photography: Tony Baker

Am I Invisible... or What?

in*visi*girl

The Crash.

8:25 The five-minute warning bell echoes through the hall. I slam my locker and squeeze through the crowd. Apparently the head cheerleader has the same path because she crashes into me, spilling both our notebooks all over the floor.

"Watch out, freshman!" she yells. I decide this is not the time to mention that I'm a sophomore.

"Sorry," I mumble as I retrieve the contents of our notebooks. She snatches her things from my hand, rolls her eyes, and walks away.

The Betrayal.

9:30 I slide into second period English, just as the bell rings. Mrs. Hammond wastes no time.

"Pair-up for a group project. You'll be working together the rest of this unit."

I frantically look around. On the other side of the room, my friend Katie avoids making eye contact with me as she partners with another girl. My only option is to ask the smelly boy who sits in front of me.

"Hey Denis, want to be partners?" He turns and grins, revealing a mouthful of braces. "Sorry, Amanda, I'm working with Hailey on this one."

I want to burst into tears. Surely Denis didn't get picked before me!

I await the inevitable. Mrs. Hammond quiets the class and asks if everyone has a partner. Mortified, I raise my hand.

"Well, whose group can Amber join?" Mrs. Hammond asks. "It's Amanda," I remind her, but I don't think she hears me. Finally I join Denis and Hailey as the only three-person group in the class.

The Put-down.

11:30 I stand in the long lunch line and try to spot my friends. One by one the students in front of me tell the cafeteria lady they want "the usual," which, since the beginning of time, means pizza and fries. When it's my turn to order I follow the pattern and order "the usual."

She shakes her pea-filled ice-cream scoop in my direction and scolds, "Honey, you're a freshman. How am I supposed to know what your 'usual' is?" Kids around me snicker.

The Hand-off.

12:45 Biology class is almost over when, to my surprise, Craig Lawrence, the most popular guy in school, sits down behind me and says, "Hey, Audrey." *Close enough,* I tell myself as my cheeks grow red. Craig leans in; my heart pounds. "Hey, do you know Marcie Fisher?" My heart sinks. *No, I don't know the homecoming queen* I want to say. Instead

I answer, "Yeah, I have Spanish with her sixth period."

"Do you think you could give her this for me?" He pulls out a note folded heart-shaped style. I nod, and shove it in my biology book.

The Forgotten.

3:30 Time for "Fiddler on the Roof" auditions. We sit in the auditorium while the directors call each girl to the audition room. I've been practicing for weeks, so I know the songs by heart. I wait for my name to be called. One by one the girls around me are summoned. Almost an hour passes, and soon I'm the only girl left. I tell myself going last is a good thing. About 30 more minutes pass, and I get nervous.

Finally I make my way to the audition room to see if something is wrong. The lights are off, and the door is closed. A large sign taped to the window reads, *Results will be posted first thing tomorrow. Don't forget to mark your name off the list after your audition.*

I feel sick. I scan the list of names, searching for Amanda Turner. I run my finger past the names of Laura Stevenson, Samantha Sullivan, and Jessica Wagner—all marked off. Then it hits me. I didn't get to audition because they left my name off the list. Like everyone else, they had completely forgotten me.

The Dis.

5:15 Mom finally arrives at school to pick me up. She waves her distracted greeting while she frantically reviews the day's meetings with the person on the other end of her cell phone. We pull into the driveway as she hangs up. "How was your day, sweetie?" she asks, as she dials a new number. "Fine," I reply as I gather my books.

The Hurt.

9:00 When I open my biology book to begin my home-work, Craig's note falls out. I completely forgot to give it to Marcie!

I stare at the heart-shaped letter, my curiosity burning. *No, Amanda, don't read someone else's letter.* But I can't help myself. I slowly unfold the note, careful to pay attention so I can return it to the heart-shape fold. The note simply reads:

Hey Marcie,
What's up? You look hott today! A bunch of us are going to Bryan's after school. Wanna come? I can take you home if you want. —Craig

One by one my tears fall, smearing Craig's note. I try to stop, but can't. No one has ever called me hott or invited me to a party. I'm the invisible girl. Always forgotten. Always overlooked. Always left out. Even my parents don't really see me.

I sob silently into my pillow.
Will anyone ever notice me? ❧

Whats Your IQ?

INVISIBILITY QUOTIENT

Answer these questions to find out how you show up in the crowd.

Which best describes you in a group?

On the fringes; chillin' in the background.

With which "Cinderella" character do you relate?

Just one of the girls.

What would hurt your feelings more?

The center of attention; the party diva.

An important member; a team player.

Cinderella, of course!

My best friend is mad at me.

Someone forgot my birthday.

How do you usually act when someone hurts you?

I'd rather avoid the conflict.

If your crush asked you out, how would you react?

I'd be blown away, shocked that he noticed me.

Which words best describe your personality?

I stand up for myself!

Let the person know how I feel—in a nice way.

I'd think, *It's about time!*

I'd feel excited and surprised.

Unique; I want to stand out from the crowd.

People-pleaser; I'm the dependable friend.

If you tried out for the school play, which role would you get?

Supporting actress.

Other girls get noticed quicker than I do.

How often do you feel like just a "face in the crowd"?

The leading lady.

False.

True.

Sometimes.

A lot.

"Shining Star"

It sounds like you have great self-confidence. You don't have a problem being noticed. You should be careful, though, not to soak up too much of the spotlight and come across as being full of yourself. It's OK to step back from being the center of attention sometimes and give other girls a chance to shine.

"Balanced Beam"

Your confidence has its ups and downs, depending on the situation. Getting noticed probably doesn't surprise you, but you don't think of yourself as a drama queen either. You have leadership qualities, but you also can follow easily. Take a stand when you really need to and keep up the balanced approach.

"Diamond in the Rough"

Whoa, girl! Lift up that chin so your beauty can be seen! Your sweet personality and dependability make you an awesome friend. But if you feel invisible, ask yourself what's getting in your way.

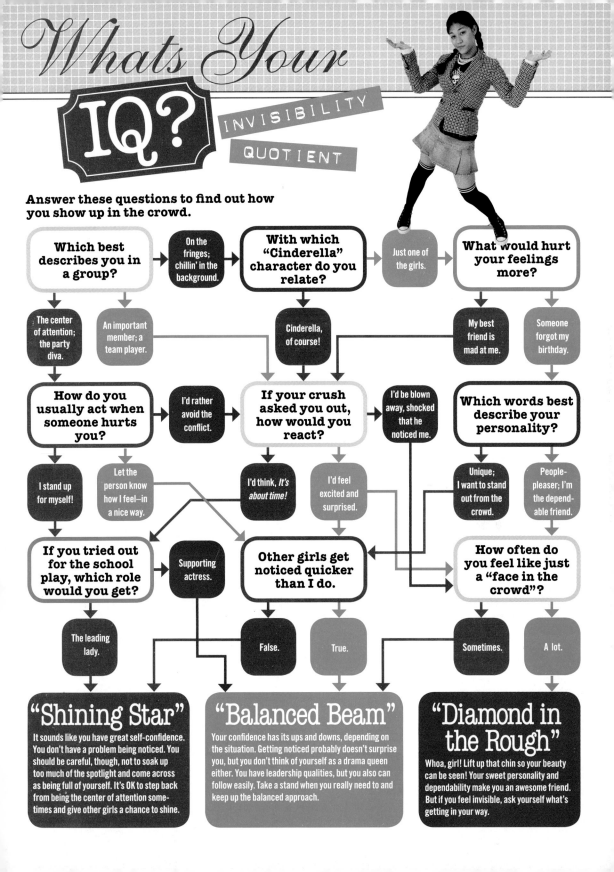

Just Like Me

I Am

I am a book with an interesting story.
I wonder if anyone will ever care to read me.
I hear someone coming to pick me up…
No, he chooses my best friend to read.
I want, just once, for someone to look inside me.
I am a book with an interesting story.

I feel as if I am alone.
Am I the only one undiscovered?
I cry out to be read, but no one hears me.
I am a book with an interesting story.

I understand the facts of life, and what life
    a book might have.
I dream that, someday, I will be seen.
I try my best to stand tall and proud.
I hope that someone will notice me.
I am a book with an interesting story.

—Kristi, 15

Can you relate to this poem? Like Kristi, maybe you believe that no one has ever really noticed you. You've learned to pretend that it's OK, that it doesn't matter. But it's not OK. And it does matter! It matters in your soul and in the way you wake up every morning.

The question is, how are you going to respond to this longing in your soul to be noticed, to be loved, to be called gorgeous?

"PLEASE! NOTICE ME!"

You were made to be seen and known and deeply loved. The question is, how are you going to respond to this longing in your soul to be noticed, to be loved, to be called gorgeous?

Girls deal with the need to be noticed in different ways. Some dress inappropriately, showing lots of skin to make sure the guys (and other people) notice. Some girls pierce holes here, there, and everywhere. Others spend tons of money on their hair, clothes, and nails to make sure they look perfect. Some even have plastic surgery to fix a "problem" with their physical appearance.

ASK YOURSELF:
> WHY AM I GETTING 'STRAIGHT A'S?
> AM I AFRAID TO MAKE A MISTAKE?
> WHY AM I HANGING OUT WITH THIS GROUP?
> AM I TRYING TO GET ATTENTION BY SHOCKING OTHERS?
> WHY AM I SHOWING SO MUCH SKIN?
> AM I TRYING TO GET GUYS TO LOOK AT ME?

Other girls try to quiet that longing in their hearts by hanging out with a dangerous crowd, even doing illegal stuff that could land them in jail—or in the morgue. Others play the "good girl," striving for perfect grades and perfect behavior. Some refuse to eat. Others are bullies.

You're Not Alone

Is it wrong to want supercute clothes or to try to get good grades? Is it wrong to want a boyfriend or a good figure? No. The problem comes when you take those desires to extremes.

You're not the only girl who feels invisible. Other girls feel invisible, too. In fact, even people in the Bible felt alone, left out, and forgotten.

Lost in the Crowd

In the New Testament, there's a story about a woman who probably felt invisible. Read Luke 8:43-48 to learn more about her.

While He was going, the crowds were nearly crushing Him. A woman suffering from bleeding for 12 years, who had spent all she had on doctors yet could not be healed by any, approached from behind and touched the tassel of His robe. Instantly her bleeding stopped.

"Who touched Me?" Jesus asked.

When they all denied it, Peter said, "Master, the crowds are hemming You in and pressing against You."

"Somebody did touch Me," said Jesus. "I know that power has gone out from Me."

When the woman saw that she was discovered, she came trembling and fell down before Him. In the presence of all the people,

she declared the reason she had touched Him and how she was instantly cured.

"Daughter," He said to her, "your faith has made you well. Go in peace"
(Luke 8:42-48).

Living as an Invisible

We don't know this woman's name, but we do know she lived in a strict Jewish culture in which her medical condition made her an outcast. She wasn't allowed to go to church, couldn't be intimate with her husband, and couldn't hang out with her friends. She had been that way for 12 years! No birthday parties. No hugs. No meals with her family. She was so lonely! She was so miserable that she was willing to spend all of her money to find a cure, but no one could heal her.

Can you imagine how desperate this woman felt? No one had hugged her in years! Everyone pretended she was invisible. Think about that for a moment. If you were her, how would you have felt?

Use this space to write a journal entry as if you were that woman. Write how you would have felt the day before you decided to find this Teacher-Healer Jesus.

You're not the only girl who feels invisible. Other girls feel invisible, too. In fact, even people in the Bible felt alone, left out, and forgotten.

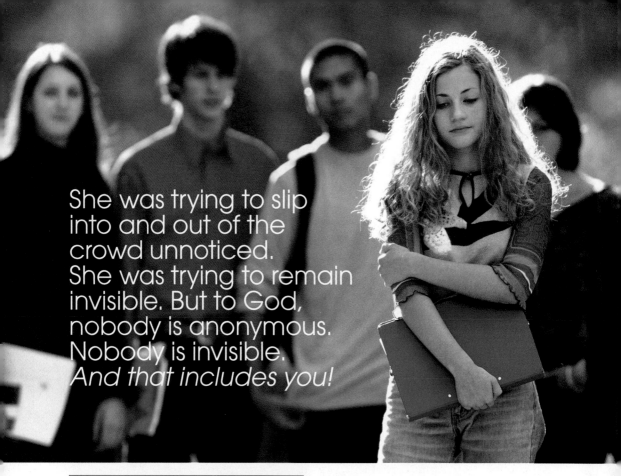

She was trying to slip into and out of the crowd unnoticed. She was trying to remain invisible. But to God, nobody is anonymous. Nobody is invisible. *And that includes you!*

✳ GET NOTICED

These tips will help people see the real you.

1. Smile. It instantly lets others know you're approachable and that you find them interesting.
2. Make the first move by asking a question. You'll be surprised by how many other teens want to get to know you. They may just be too shy, or they may actually be intimidated by you. (Imagine that!)
3. What do you love to do? Find other girls who like to do the same thing.
4. Ask yourself what your body language is saying to others. Crossed arms scream, "Stay away from me!" Trade this negative body language for a positive move: look others in the eye when you're talking to them—and maintain that eye contact while they speak.
5. Be honest. Tell your parents if their actions make you feel invisible. Offer specific suggestions for small changes that will make a big difference.

Invisible No More

This woman must have been petrified around that crowd of people. However, when you're feeling alone and forgotten, you'll do what it takes. Notice what happened after she touched Jesus' robe. *He noticed.* He asked who touched Him. And it scared the woman.

> *Then the woman, seeing that she could not go unnoticed, came trembling and fell at his feet (Luke 8:47, NIV).*

Did you catch that? She was trying to slip into and out of the crowd unnoticed. She was trying to remain invisible. She was used to it. After all this time, nobody paid attention to her. But she was encountering no ordinary person; she was encountering God. And to God, nobody is anonymous. Nobody is invisible. And that includes you!✳

You Are Not Invisible.

SEE

Confessions of a Former "Mean Girl"

By Rachel Armstrong with Marie Armenia

There were three of us, and we made a good team. We looked good together: one short, cute, blue-eyed blonde; a killer red-head; and me—the long-legged brunette. We were popular and good at putting everybody else down. I could talk with a smile on my face and say something like, "Oh, Britney, you look so pretty today!" Then I would turn around and roll my eyes. I'd lie and manipulate my way through the day. So would my girlfriends. Manipulation was a big rush for us.

> **I didn't really want the guy, but I didn't want her to have him either. So I just took him from her.**

Even though we were mean, we were popular. Everybody wanted to be one of us. I remember one girl who wanted to be a part of "the group." One day at school she had this medicine that numbed her mouth because she'd recently had her wisdom teeth removed. There was this teacher who didn't like our group, so we were out to get her. She was always chugging water during class. (That woman could drink!) So I took this girl's numbing medicine and put it all around the rim of that teacher's cup. At the beginning of class, as usual, our teacher started chugging her water.

After a while she started talking funny, like there was something stuck on the roof of her mouth, you know? We were ripping about it! That girl with the medicine took the fall for it and got suspended for three days for trying to poison a teacher.

Another time there was this girl who was my friend, kinda. Anyway, she was dating this guy, OK? And they broke up. Right after they broke up, I saw him at a football game. I was talking to him, you know, and we exchanged phone numbers.

Then later I was just like, "He's not for me. I can do better!" And basically what went down was he and that girl started talking again.

The next week someone said to me, "Rachel, I thought you were talking to him?" And so immediately I went into "mine" mode, you know? I didn't really want the guy, but I didn't want her to have him either.

So I just took him from her.

The girl didn't come from a good home life. She'd had it rough, like all the time, and she tried so hard to get that guy back. Eventually—and this is the part that really kills me—she did get him back because she slept with him. That's what she thought she had to do, I guess, to beat me. But she didn't keep him….

See page 54 for the rest of my story.

MANIPULATION
WAS
A BIG RUSH
FOR US.

When do you feel the most invisible?

left out of the group

unwanted?

"Sometimes I feel completely invisible at church and don't want to go to youth group because I don't know if there will be anybody there I can sit with." —Meagan, 17

"In middle school, the cheerleaders always hang out with other cheer-leaders. They don't notice anyone else." —Tori, 13

self-concious

"All the jocks will be standing around in the hallway. I get really self-conscious, so I just pick up my cell phone and pretend to be talking to someone so they won't notice me." —Andrea, 15

✳ instant message

To God, nobody is invisible. You were made to be seen and known and loved deeply. And it's OK to want what you were made for.

Describe a moment in your life when you felt invisible (or wished you were).

innergirl

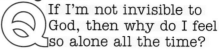

plain & simple

Q I'm plain looking, don't make great grades, and don't have any cool friends. Why should I think I'm NOT invisible?

A What if you could hear the audible voice of God? What if you could hear Him speak? Would you believe Him? If you could hear His voice, then you'd hear God tell you He sees you every single minute.

God never takes His eyes off you. He even stands guard while you sleep (Ps. 121:4). He will always be with you (Matt. 28:20). He calls you beautiful, and you are His beloved (Ps. 45:11).

When you feel invisible, that usually means that you don't believe you qualify for the popular crowd. Feeling left out always hurts, but what you need is some perspective. The God of heaven and earth is wild about you! He sees your heart and feels your pain. You have never, not even for a second, been invisible to Him.

In Isaiah 55:8-9 God says that His thoughts are not our thoughts and His ways are not our ways. Whatever He is thinking and doing matters more than what this week's "in" girls have decided is cool.

So what would happen if you began to act like God is wild about you? Would you let that truth lift your spirit and make your heart come alive? According to worldly standards, you may feel invisible. But that could never be true with God.

> When you feel invisible, that usually means that you don't believe you qualify for the popular crowd.

being alone

Q If I'm not invisible to God, then why do I feel so alone all the time?

A Unfortunately, loneliness is an unavoidable part of being a human. Every person on the planet knows what it's like to be lonely. You were created for relationships. While we're here on earth, we're going to have some great relationships. Many times, the people we love will be wonderful to us; sometimes they can be disappointing, or even hurtful. And when there's no one, or no one we desire to be with, the heart is lonely and longs for more.

Until we stand in God's presence, each one of us will battle different kinds of loneliness. It's lonely to be home alone—without a date or a fun girlfriend who can help you laugh the night away. It's lonely to be misunderstood by your parents or teacher. Your heart was made for acceptance and perfect communication.

When I feel lonely, I try to let that feeling remind me of heaven. I was made for heaven. I was made for perfect relationship, and it's still to come. Loneliness helps me remember that I'm just passing through on my way to the One who is Perfect Love.

Angela Thomas is crazy about her four teenage and preteen kids. She is a great carpool driver, baseball watcher, and flat-iron stylist. When the kids can't think of anything else for her to do, she writes books for women and speaks at events around the country. www.angelathomas.com

REAL *Love*

by S. Moen

Flashing lights. Loud voices. Smoke. She felt a mask cover her face. Finally, cool air.

When Rachel opened her eyes, dimmed lights welcomed her. The peaceful silence was interrupted by a softly spoken greeting.

"I'm glad you're awake. How do you feel?" Rachel turned her head to see a nurse. "I'm not sure," she replied. Her voice cracked, and it hurt to talk.

"You'll feel better in a few days."

"Where are my parents?"

"Your mother is just outside." The nurse opened the door and motioned. Rachel saw her mother's face come into focus.

"I'm OK, Mom." Rachel's mother took a deep breath and kissed her forehead. "Where's Dad?" Rachel asked.

"Daddy's … not here, Sweetie. When the house caught on fire, he ran upstairs to your room. Then he covered your body with his and walked through the fire. He got you out, but his injuries were too severe."

"Daddy's dead?" Rachel barely spoke the question as she felt the room darken. She thought she would fall down even though she was lying in the hospital bed.

A week later Rachel stared at her home, which was draped in ugly, blue tarps. An acrid burnt smell still lingered. Rachel knew her father was dead, but everything around her was alive with his presence. She saw him in the backyard hammock, where he loved to nap on Sunday afternoons. She

> RACHEL KNEW HER FATHER WAS DEAD, BUT EVERYTHING AROUND HER WAS ALIVE WITH HIS PRESENCE.

saw him beside the goofy fish mailbox he had installed one Saturday morning. And she saw him smiling through the window of his beat-up, red Volkswagon bug. She was about to cry when her mother took her by the arm and led her to the swing in the back yard.

"I found a letter Daddy wrote to you."

"Really?" Rachel took the letter and began to read her dad's big scrawl.

"Hey, Little Princess. I just left your room; you were sleeping like a baby, all snuggled in. So beautiful. I said a prayer for you while you slept. Princess, I want you to have this letter so you'll never forget that my love for you goes on and on. Ever since I knew you were going to be born, I loved you. From the moment I held you in my arms, you were the sunshine in my day. I'm proud to say I survived your dirty diapers (although, to be honest, it was touch-and-go at times). And I was always tickled when you put your little hand in mine, even after

God could not have given me a better present than to have a daughter like you. Every time I think of you, I thank Him that you were born.

If you are reading this, it means that I can't tell you these things anymore. But always remember that I'll never stop loving you. I'm putting you in God's hands now, and I know He will care for you far better than I could. You can trust Him. Always.

I love you Princess, Dad"

Rachel's face was streaming with tears. "There's one more thing. It's a Bible verse.

'This is my command: love one another as I have loved you. No one has greater love than this, that someone would lay down his life for his friends.' John 15:12-13.

Dad added the note, 'He did it for me.'"

Rachel moved closer to her mother and put her arm around her. "We're lucky, aren't we, Mom? We both get to know what love really means." ✳

your finger had spent time in your turned-up nose. **Lately, I've watched you grow into a beautiful teenager.** *Maybe you didn't notice because you were so busy with your friends and the things you love, but I was always watching over you. You will always be my little Sugar Britches.*

✳ WHAT IS TRUE LOVE?

List what you think are the qualities of true love.

❶ Someone who really loves me will _____
_____

❷ Someone who really loves me will never _____
_____

❸ True love is _____
_____

My World
7days

memorize Luke 8:47

1

"Then the woman, seeing that she could not go unnoticed, came trembling and fell at his feet" (Luke 8:47, NIV).

✱ Things to do this week to remind yourself you're not invisible.

don't waste time
Turn off the TV this week. Spend that time alone with God.

2

look up
Make eye contact with others this week.

3

forgive me!
Apologize to someone you have treated as invisible.

4

find a new friend
Sit with someone in the cafeteria who may feel invisible.

5

talk with your parents
Share what makes you feel invisible and what makes you feel important.

6

self-talk
Write the following on a colorful piece of paper and mount it near your mirror: "I, _____, am not invisible!"

7

Note to me: Don't forget to look someone in the eye today.

In My Own Words

One physical feature that makes me stand out is

I think these people feel invisible

I tend to treat these people as if they are invisible

A Bible verse that reminds me I'm not invisible is

A personal story that reminds me I'm not invisible is

FIND TRUTH.

know
HIM
There is no substitute.

An Eye for Beauty

by Jennifer Wilson

I had a greater chance of being struck by lightning than going to prom.

i was eating fries and trying not to get ketchup on my shirt, when I saw David McCaman, the hottest guy in school, stand to return his lunch tray. David always sat with his football and cheerleader friends. We had geometry together, but we lived in different worlds.

In my universe, I wasn't popular or unpopular—I wasn't anything. I wasn't pretty enough to be noticed or smart enough to be "gifted." I just sorta blended in. Well, I did have one special feature: I was clumsy. I was always spilling my drink, tripping, and slamming my locker on someone's fingers. If I made it through the day without giving myself or anyone else a bruise, it was a great day.

As I stuffed a ketchup-drenched fry into my mouth, David walked over and sat right beside me. No joke! All my friends became really interested in their food. They pretended not to notice that the captain of the football team had descended from Mount Popular into nerd land. I squeaked out a barely intelligible, "Hi."

David smiled his prince charming smile and said, "Hey, Jen. You're in my geometry class, right?"

My insides screamed, *Come on Jen, for once in your life, say something cool.* Instead, I squeezed out a "Yep," nodding like a yo-yo for added nerd effect. After an awkward silence, David said, "Well, you know prom is coming up."

I pretended to know, but really I hadn't paid attention. Sophomores weren't allowed to go unless a senior asked them. That meant I had a greater chance of being struck by lightning than going to prom. To my astonishment, lightning struck.

"Um, would you go with me?"

I must have looked at David like his face was mutating, because he quickly added, "It's cool, if you don't want to go."

The floor swayed beneath me, but I managed to say, "That sounds great!" David smiled, stood, and sauntered back into the popular mist. After the feeling returned to my limbs, it hit me: *David McCaman just asked me—a nobody—to the prom!*

The next day David began walking me to my classes. He actually gave up sitting with his cheerleader friends at lunch to sit with mine every day! I started to feel important, even pretty. David told me I was beautiful, but in the back of my mind a

voice kept saying, *Come on, Jen, you don't deserve this! You're not popular or pretty; one day this all will end.* I told David how I felt, and he said I needed to believe in myself, to believe I am beautiful.

"It doesn't matter what anyone else thinks, Jen," he said. "You're amazing just the way you are." And then I did something very unlike me. I believed him!

Suddenly I had confidence. I was beautiful, and it didn't matter that I wasn't a cheerleader. I spoke out in class, even if others disagreed with me. I boldly asked some of the football players to stop picking on the freshmen. I didn't have to blend in anymore. I could be who I was. I mattered! I was beautiful to David, so I became beautiful to myself.

Seeing myself through David's eyes changed me. I learned to love myself for who I was, even if David wasn't around. Did I still sit with my nerdy friends? Of course. Did I still dribble ketchup all over myself? Pretty much every day. But I could finally trip down the hallway with joy knowing that I was loved, admired, and beautiful just because I was me. ❀

> And then I did something very unlike me. I believed him!

✳ DON'T BUY THE LIES

When you think about that guy you really crush on, do you find yourself asking:
Will you love me if...
> I SLEEP WITH YOU?
> DO DRUGS WITH YOU?
> LIE FOR YOU?
> PROP YOU UP?
Any guy who puts conditions on his love doesn't have an eye for your beauty. He's only thinking of himself! Lose him FAST!

Pop Quiz

What Does God See When He Looks at Me?

Do you believe what God *says* about you? Take this quiz to find out.

1. God is probably irritated with me most of the time. T/F
2. I think God cares about the big picture, but not every detail or problem in my life. T/F
3. I've messed up too much for God to let me start over. T/F
4. When God looks at me, He *sees* what everyone else *sees*. T/F
5. God knows everything about me and loves me anyway. T/F
6. God wants to be close to me. T/F
7. God thinks I'm beautiful. T/F
8. God wants good things for me. T/F
9. God doesn't understand the stuff I have to deal with. T/F
10. God really listens when I pray. T/F

ANSWERS:

1. **False.** OK, so you do mess up sometimes. It does bother God when you do, especially when you know better; but He would rather you honestly try to please Him, even if you fail. Just read about King David in the Bible. He messed up, too.
2. **False.** God does care about the big picture, but He also wants to be involved in every detail and decision in your life. He wants to rescue you from pain like your very own knight in shining armor. He even knows how many hairs are on your head! He delights in you! Don't believe it? Read Psalm 18:16-19 and Matthew 10:29-31.
3. **False.** God is willing to forgive you an unlimited amount of times, but you need to be sincere when you ask Him. He also wants you to stop making the same bad choices over and over again. Read Psalm 51 and 1 John 1:9.
4. **False.** God sees you more completely than any human being can. He created you! He cares about you—inside and out!
5. **True.** Read Psalm 139.
6. **True.** You exist to have a relationship with God. Isn't that amazing?
7. **True.** Check out Psalm 45:10-11.
8. **True.** God wants you to be happy (in the right ways). Read Jeremiah 29:11 and Matthew 7:7-12.
9. **False.** OK, so maybe Jesus didn't go through a nasty break-up, but He does know what it feels like to be ignored, lied about, made fun of, betrayed, spit on, misunderstood by His parents, and abandoned by His friends. Read any story about His life (in Matthew, Mark, Luke, or John) and also read Hebrews 4:14-16 to understand more.
10. **True.** You'll find proof all over the Bible. Read Psalm 145:17-19 for one example.

Deeper

Hey! God is Wild About You!

Have you ever asked yourself, *Does anyone see me? Will anyone ever call me gorgeous?* Maybe you've bought into the lie that you'll never be pretty enough, tall enough, smart enough, unique enough, or important enough.

Maybe you've bought into the lie that you'll never be pretty enough, tall enough, smart enough, unique enough, or important enough.

You look at everyone around you and think, *There's no way I can compete. My sister is smarter. My best friend is prettier. My teammates are better players.*

But here's some great news: The God who slung the stars across heavens … whose very breath gives life … that God, the King, has always been taken with you. He thinks you're gorgeous. In fact, He is absolutely wild about you!

When God looks at you, He sees all the beauty He created. He sees every potential. Every gift. He loves the curly hair that you wish were straight. He loves your smile and the shape of your nose. He's crazy about big feet and wobbly knees and every curve that you wish would go away. He loves the inside and outside of you. After all, you were His idea! You are physically and emotionally BEAUTIFUL to Him. Check out the verses in the blue box below that scream of God's love for you.

You're probably thinking, *OK. That's great. God is enthralled with me. What does that really mean?*

Wowed by Words

LISTEN, O DAUGHTER, DON'T MISS A WORD: FORGET YOUR PEOPLE AND YOUR FATHER'S HOUSE. THE KING IS *ENTHRALLED BY YOUR BEAUTY;* HONOR HIM, FOR HE IS YOUR LORD.
—PSALM 45:10-11, NIV (Emphasis Added)

Circle all the words below that are synonyms of the word *enthralled.* Then put a star by the word you like the most.

bored	head over heels
abusive	aloof
spellbound	displeased
thrilled	captivated
wild about	disgusted
indifferent	delighted
wowed	fascinated
possessive	disappointed
drawn to	mesmerized

The God
who slung
the stars
across
heavens ...
whose very
breath gives
life ... that God,
the King, has
always been
taken with you.
He thinks you're
GORGEOUS
In fact, He is
absolutely
wild about you!

Does it seem strange to think that God is enthralled with you? In fact, Psalm 45:11 can be translated as, "The king is wild for you!" *(THE MESSAGE)*

Does it seem strange to think that God is enthralled with you? In fact, Psalm 45:11 can be translated as, "The king is wild for you!" (*THE MESSAGE*)

Wild about you? **Yes!**

Who will fight for you? God.
Who will never leave you? God.
Who calls you beautiful? God.
Why? Because He's wild about you!

There's a lot in the Bible about how God feels about you. In each of the following boxes is a Scripture passage. Look up each passage in your Bible, then describe what each tells you about God's feelings toward you.

Psalm 139:13-16

Isaiah 43:1-4

Ephesians 3:17-19

Isaiah 63:9

Isaiah 49:14-16

Inside and Out

You've probably heard the story of Mary, the mother of Jesus. Mary was engaged to Joseph when an angel came to her and announced she would give birth to Jesus, the Messiah, the One who would redeem Israel and the rest of humanity. The greeting the angel gave Mary is something to focus on for a minute. In *The Message*, Eugene Peterson paraphrases Luke 1:28.

"Good morning! You're beautiful with God's beauty, Beautiful inside and out!"

And guess what? God feels the exact same way about you. In fact, you could fill in the blank using your name, and the Scripture would apply.

"GOOD MORNING,

_____!

(fill in your name)

YOU'RE BEAUTIFUL WITH GOD'S BEAUTY, BEAUTIFUL INSIDE AND OUT! NOT JUST A NUMBER.

You may be saying to yourself, *Yeah, He loves me. But He just loves me like He's loved every other created person in the history of the universe. I'm just one among zillions!*

If you think that, then hear this:

God's love for you is not just some kind of blanket love.

It's more than a pat on the head for being a good girl or a zap with a lightning bolt when you mess up. His love sees into your soul and can hold you with a power and strength greater than you could ever imagine. You are His, and He is yours. You belong to Him!

How do you feel knowing that God loves you with this kind of intensity?

Remember, God loves you with an intense, knock-you-off-your-feet kind of love that's unique and just for you. You're not just one among zillions. That's just how big and great God's love is. And He's wild about you! ❀

out

of

the

blue

by Bethany Hamilton

My plans to be a professional surfer got hit pretty hard Halloween morning of 2003. It came, literally, out of the blue. I had no warning at all; not even the slightest hint of danger.... The water was crystal clear and calm....

The waves were small and inconsistent, and I was just kind of rolling along with them, relaxing on my board with my right hand on the nose of the board and my left arm dangling in the cool water … when suddenly there was a flash of gray.

These people like me for who I am: one arm, two arms, or no arms; it doesn't matter.

That's all it took: a split second. I felt a lot of pressure and a couple of lightning-fast tugs. I couldn't make out any of the details, but I knew that the huge jaws of a 15-foot tiger shark covered the top of my board and my left arm. Then I watched in shock as the water around me turned bright red. Somehow, I stayed calm and started to paddle toward the beach. My left arm was gone almost to the armpit, along with a huge, crescent-shaped chunk of my red-white-and-blue surfboard.... I wasn't freaking out, but I was praying like crazy, "Please, God, help me. Let me get to the beach."

In the weeks and months that followed [the shark attack] I had a lot of [healing] to do. Often, it was scary or trying. I won't lie to you: in some ways it still is.

But for me, knowing that God loves me and that He has a plan for my life that no shark can take away is like having solid rock underneath me. Look, lots of bad stuff happens to people. That's life. And here's my advice: don't put all your hope and faith into something that could suddenly and easily disappear. And honestly, that's almost anything. The only thing that will never go away, that will never fail you, is your faith in God.

I have been blessed in my life. People ask me, "How can you say that after this horrible thing happened to you?" Because I have to look at the big picture: I have a family that loves me and encourages me to go after my dreams. I have a big *ohana* of Christian friends from the community and the surf world that care about me. And I have close personal friends. These people like me for who I am: one arm, two arms, or no arms; it doesn't matter.

But most of all, I have a relationship with Christ that keeps me strong and helps me see how good can come out of a bad situation. I think the reason I haven't gotten all bummed out about losing my arm is due to God. I think that the reason I have been able to tell my story on TV and in magazines is because God wanted other people to know that He is the rock you can build your life on.

I think this was God's plan for me all along. I'm not saying that God *made* the shark bite me. I think He knew it would happen, and He made a way for my life to be happy and meaningful *in spite* of it. God knows what's going on and will make good come from bad. If I can help other people find hope in God, then that is worth losing my arm.

> **I'm not saying that God made the shark bite me. I think He knew it would happen, and He made a way for my life to be happy and meaningful in spite of it.**

My friend Sarah says I get to be the voice of God. I usually roll my eyes when she says it, because if I were God, I would never have chosen me, of all people, to speak for Him! But for reasons I don't understand, at least for a while, He has chosen me to say what He wants people to know: that He is real, that He loves them, that they can know Him and trust Him. Maybe He picked me because I tell it like it is: I don't know how to sound smart or sophisticated in interviews. I just say what's in my heart and hopefully my mouth cooperates!

And I am thankful. I could have died. I could have really been mangled. I could have been hurt so bad that I might not have been able to surf again. I have lots and lots to be thankful for.

I really don't want people looking to me for inspiration. I just want to

be a sign along the way that points toward heaven. I think Jeremiah 29:11 is for every [girl] who is feeling down or defeated or a little lost in life, perhaps angry or frustrated by what's going on: *"For I know the plans I have for you,"* declares the LORD, *"plans to prosper you and not to harm you, plans to give you hope and a future."* (NIV)

I'm proud to be part of God's plans, and I hope, in some small way, this surfer girl can make Him proud, too.❁

Bethany won her FIRST NATIONAL TITLE—she's the 2005 NSSA Explorer Women's Champion! For updates on Bethany visit *www.bethanyhamilton.com*.

Excerpted and adapted with permission of MTV Books/Pocket Books, an imprint of Simon & Schuster Adult Publishing Group, from *SOUL SURFER: A True Story of Faith, Family, and Fighting to Get Back on the Board* by Bethany Hamilton with Sheryl Berk and Rick Bundschuh. Copyright © 2004 by Bethany Hamilton.

believe

God has great plans for you!

VIEW

Does God REALLY think I am beautiful?

"God, do You really see me in all this mess and still call me beautiful? Even when my breath is not minty-fresh, and my hair looks gross? Do You really love me in spite of my flaws?"

*instant message

And God replies...
"If you could only grasp how wide and how high and how deep, then _____ (insert your name), you'd know, I really love you."

too far away?

"Do you wonder if you are too far away from Me? My love is still wider. Do you think that you've been away too long? My love will wait longer. Do you believe that no one would ever want someone like you? My love is higher than all the others. Have you been sure that you are too far gone?"

"My love is deep enough to reach even you. You cannot fall past My love. You cannot outrun My love. You cannot reach the end of My love. It is wide and long and high and deep enough for you."

This is enduring, unfailing love…the completing love your heart longs for!

Why is it so hard to accept that you are beautiful just as you are?

good enough?

"All you see on TV are gorgeous people. It's so easy to say to yourself 'I'm not good enough because I'm not as pretty as they are.' " —Allison, 16

You are no mistake!

"Images of perfect bodies are everywhere. Girls see them and try to aspire to something that isn't real. But God made each of us in His image. If you think you are ugly, then you must think God is ugly. But He does not make mistakes!" —Erica, 21

Ask Angela

hard to believe

Q Honestly, I'm just not sure about this whole beautiful thing. I don't think I could ever believe that about myself. Does anybody else feel that way?

A You sound like almost every other girl I have talked to. But here's the deal: in Psalm 45:11, God says to me and to you and every single one of your girlfriends, "The king is enthralled with your beauty."

God sees you and calls you beautiful. And in case you need to be reminded, every time God says something, it's true.

So right this very minute, wherever you are and no matter how you feel about yourself, God is speaking that truth over you. He is always calling your name, always pursuing your heart, continually wanting you to hear and believe that His love for you can never be changed.

Think about it. What if you decided in this moment to believe that God calls you beautiful? That one, huge idea could radically change your whole life. What if you acted and responded like God is wild about you? What if you staked your whole life on it? And then what if you began to live inside the blessings that come to a girl when she begins to believe and live the truth of God?

Even if you don't believe it, the Bible says that God calls you beautiful. Every day you refuse to embrace His love is another day far away from the life He dreamed for you.

greater love

Q Angela, How can I believe in God's love when I can't see Him? It's not like He can give me a hug when I'm down.

A There are a couple of great reasons to believe in God's love. First, over and over in the Bible, He tells us that His love endures. You are His created. Your mind, your body, and even the way you laugh were all His idea. Before you were ever born, God was in love with you. And His love for you will never fail. (See Ps. 136.)

The other reason to believe in God's love is that He sent His only Son, Jesus, to save you from the punishment of sin. You don't send your only Son for someone you just like a little. You send your only Son for the ones you passionately love.

Did you know God sends messengers? When you need a hug or an encouraging word, pray and ask Him. Then look for His answer. He sends hugs through friends and family. When you are looking for the love of God, you will be amazed to see how He sends it. Sometimes we have to learn how to hear His voice and practice watching for His ways.

> When you need a hug or an encouraging word, pray and ask Him. Then look for His answer. He sends hugs through friends and family.

Angela Thomas is crazy about her four teenage and preteen kids. She is a great carpool driver, baseball watcher, and flat-iron stylist. When the kids can't think of anything else for her to do, she writes books for women and speaks at events around the country. www.angelathomas.com

It's not what's outside that matters to me.
What really counts is that you

Shine!

BY S. MOEN

Paige groaned as she followed her mom. "It won't take long, so come on." The bedroom floor was covered with stuff Paige's Grandma had saved forever.

"I'll sort out the things we'll keep, and you take the rest downstairs."

Five minutes later, Paige trudged down the stairs to dump the musty-smelling clothes. *Gross,* Paige thought as she headed back up.

Her mother was sorting through boxes. Paige opened a shoebox she found near an old lamp. In it were letters bound together with a pink ribbon, which Paige carefully untied. The postmark on the first letter was more than 50 years old. She slipped it from the envelope.

My darling Helen, it began.

"Hey, Mom, these are letters to Grandma from Grandpa. They're really old."

"My darling Helen," read Paige. *"Today we're getting ready for an attack. Some of us will probably be killed, so I wanted to write to you while it's quiet."*

Paige's mother stopped working. She moved closer to Paige. "Your grandfather was in World War II."

Paige continued. *"I want to tell you how incredibly special you are to me. I know I've told you that I love you a hundred of times already, but I thought I would try to tell you why I love you so much."*

Paige and her mother sat on the bed, totally engrossed in the letter.

"Keep reading, sweetheart."

"I adore you," the letter continued.

"Every time I think about you I thank God that He wanted you to be with me. I know that it was His plan because you fill my heart with joy. It's like you know the music of my soul, and when I hold your hand or kiss you, every note is just right. There's a symphony inside you that brings out the best in me." Paige saw her mother wipe a tear.

"Every glimmer of your heart draws me toward you. You glitter like the stars in the sky. It's scary, and at the same time, irresistible. You have a peaceful center that shelters me. I remember when we sat under the big oak tree at the park. That's the kind of rest I find in you. I think Solomon got it right when he said that a man must trust his wife like he trusts God. When I put my life in your hands, I know that you'll care for me, maybe even better than I care for myself. I miss your touch so much now. No other person on earth makes me feel like you do. It's not what's outside that matters to me. This war has helped me sort out what really counts. And what really counts is that you shine! You're the wild rose I found on the hillside, made just to let me enjoy you forever. My heart longs to be with you.

Love,
Frank"

Paige looked into her mother's eyes. "Grandma was so lucky. I want someone to love me like Grandpa loved Grandma."

"Just be patient, Paige. When the time is right, God will bring the right guy into your life, and you'll shine for him. Just like your Grandma did for Grandpa." ✻

Shining Example!

List on the rings of this circle the qualities that make you shine.

My World 7days

*Things to do this week to remind yourself God thinks you're gorgeous!

1 the King is calling!

Memorize a personalized version of Psalm 45:10-11: "Now listen,
_____ (insert your name), don't miss a word … the king is wild for you." *(THE MESSAGE)*

2 Feature attraction

Ask a friend what your best feature is.

4 wise women

Spend time with an older woman. Ask her how she knows she's gorgeous.

5 you rock!

Give someone a compliment each day.

3 night moves

Read Ephesians 3:17b-19 every night before you go to bed: "And I ask him that with both feet planted firmly on love, you'll be able to take in with all Christians the extravagant dimensions of Christ's love. Reach out and experience the breadth! Test its length! Plumb the depths! Rise to the heights! Live full lives, full in the fullness of God." *(THE MESSAGE)*

6 heart of gold

Go to a nursing home. Remind an elderly woman of her beauty and value.

7 adorable

Pray Psalm 139:13-14 to God each day.
"Oh yes, you shaped me first inside, then out; you formed me in my mother's womb. I thank you, High God—you're breathtaking! Body and soul, I am marvelously made! I worship in adoration—what a creation!" *(THE MESSAGE)*

In My Own Words

I feel the most beautiful when

When I think of God being totally in love with me, I feel

Knowing that God loves me, flaws and all, makes me want to

Someone I look up to because she really knows God loves her unconditionally is

I really struggle with God being wild about me because

Someone who needs to know that God really wants a relationship with her is

The Voices of Other Loves

A good guy can be wonderful. But he can never be enough, and he can never make you whole.

What Lies Beneath

by Caroline Mitchell

When my Sunday school teacher asked us to make a list of people we needed to forgive, the first name on my list was my dad. I was 5 when he told my mom and me he was moving out. A couple of years after my parents divorced, he remarried.

When my dad and step-mother had a baby, Dad was caught up in the life of his new child; I was left out. I was angry, jealous, afraid, and hurt.

That time also sparked other realizations for me. I had known that my stepmother was a student in my dad's college minis-try. It dawned on me that my dad had an affair with her and basically abandoned my mom, my sister, and me. I was shocked that my father would do something like that.

My damaged relationship with my father affected my ability to relate to guys. I shut myself off emotionally from the guys I liked. I was scared of getting hurt.

During high school, I did lots of things to fill the hole Dad left in my life. I tried to get attention by pursuing singing, academic compe-titions—anything that made me look good. By my senior year, I was jealous of anyone who succeeded more than I did. I felt like everyone was trying intentionally to hurt me and make me fail. That made me really angry.

I thought going to college would give me a chance to start over, however, after just a few months at college, I was miserable again. Then I started hanging with a girl whose parents also were divorced. She got me to open up about my dad, and I started to see that so many things that were going wrong in my life were because of the relationship lessons I'd learned from him and carried out in my own life. My friend helped me to see my own value as a person and how I was allow-ing outside influences to make me miserable. She also helped me to see how valuable and beautiful I am in the eyes of God. I learned that everyone makes mistakes. Christ died for our mistakes because none of us can reach perfection on our own. I finally realized that looking to others for per-fection will always disappoint me.

It has taken me years to realize God has never given up on me, even if it seems my earthly father has. I don't need to hold bitterness toward Dad; he's not perfect. No one but Christ fits that bill, and the only way to find joy in this world is through faith in Jesus Christ.

Like a knight in shining armor, God has res-cued me from my past. He has forgiven me and given me the ability to forgive those who have hurt me. Sure, it hurts that I don't have a better relationship with my dad, but that loss doesn't have to define who I am. My heavenly Father is defining me anew every day. And He is all the strength and hope I could ever want.❋

> "During high school, I did lots of things to fill the hole Dad left in my life."

CHATROOM

POST SUBJECT: If you could change something about your parents, what would it be?

punkangel
I wish my parents weren't divorced.

crazeegurl9
I wish my parents would listen more than they talk. They advise, but they don't understand the situation.

beachgrl
I wish my parents had better communication skills. I love my dad and I love to talk to him, but he has a hard time listening to me. The only time he really listens to me is when I say something that has to do with him. If it's something I care about, he doesn't listen.

punkangel
I wish my parents weren't so afraid to have a mature conversation with me. They think I'm 12 and talk to me like I'm 12. I'm not a little kid.

beachgrl
I hate it when my dad tells me not to do something and then he does it.

crazeegurl9
Me too. My dad will laugh at an inappropriate commercial on TV, then I'll laugh and I'll get in trouble.

beachgrl
My dad always commits to something, and then he won't follow through. I know my dad is human, but I also know God is not! It's encouraging to know that I have a Heavenly Father I can turn to when my real dad lets me down.

THE LOVE QUIZ

Take these 3 mini-quizzes to see which love takes most of your attention.

1 BOYS

1. Which best describes you?
   a) Having a boyfriend is fun, but I'm cool without one, too.
   b) Are you kidding? Everyone thinks you're a loser without a guy.
2. When you have a boyfriend, what do your friends usually think?
   a) They're pretty cool with it.
   b) They accuse me of spending too much time with him.
3. Having a boyfriend does (or would) make me feel better about myself.
   a) Not really.
   b) Yeah, I guess I have to admit it does (or would).
4. The Bible says that God thinks you're gorgeous. What's your response?
   a) Wow!
   b) It would be easier to believe if a guy told me that.
5. I would do (or have done) things I regret to get (or keep) a boyfriend.
   a) I don't think so.
   b) Yeah, who hasn't?

How many b's did you pick? _____ [Now go to part 2.]

2 FATHER

1. When your dad gets home from work, which is he more likely to do?
   a) Say hi and give you a hug.
   b) Grab the remote and zone out.
2. I have a pretty cool relationship with my dad.
   a) Sure.
   b) Let's not go there.
3. Which sounds more like something your dad would say to you?
   a) You look pretty today.
   b) What were you thinking?
4. When you get in trouble, how does your dad handle it?
   a) Talk or lecture, or some other thing parents do.
   b) Are you kidding? I can get away with murder with my dad.
5. It's Sunday morning at your house. What's your dad probably doing?
   a) Getting ready for church.
   b) His own thing.

How many b's did you pick? _____ [Now go to part 3.]

3 FRIENDS

1. Which scene best describes shopping with your buds?
   a) I usually buy what I think is cool, with some suggestions from friends.
   b) I would never wear something my friends didn't like.
2. You just found out your friend has spread a nasty rumor about you. You:
   a) Confront her and try to talk about it.
   b) Feel so hurt and angry that you decide your life is over.
3. I've had friends say I was too clingy.
   a) No, that's not me at all.
   b) Maybe once or twice.
4. Fill in the blank: It would honestly bother me more if _____ were mad at me.
   a) God
   b) My best friend
5. I would do something I knew was wrong if my best friend pushed me to join her.
   a) No way. I'm so over that peer pressure stuff.
   b) Who wouldn't?

How many b's did you pick? _____ [Now read the directions for scoring.]

Scoring: Check your score for each mini-quiz. Which one had the most b's? Read the descriptions below to find out what that says about you. Did you have more than 2 b's on any mini-quiz? If so, check out each interpretation.

1. Boys OK, so it's normal to crush on guys, even to fall in love. It's also fine to want the attention and approval of your special guy. Just realize that it can be unhealthy to crave it so much that you base your whole self-esteem on what he says about you. Remember, God created you with a space only He can fill, and He will if you let Him!

2. Father Few girls grow up in a picture-perfect home. Most experts believe that a girl learns a lot about God from how her dad treats her. If he is loving and attentive, it's easier for the girl to see God that way. If your dad is harsh, critical, or not there for you at all, you may think God is that way, too. This is not true! Dads are supposed to give their daughters a healthy taste of God's love. But girl, if your dad doesn't, know that you have the best example of unconditional love in a relationship with your Heavenly Father. He is wild about you!

3. Friends Who doesn't love spending time with someone who knows you inside and out and can finish your sentences? It's perfectly healthy to need friends—in fact, God created you that way. But your friends were never meant to take the place of God in your life or in your heart. Remember, no friend can be everything you need. Only God can do that!

Are Other Loves Playing You?

Many girls get so distracted by boys, their dads, their friends, or other stuff (like money, clothes, sports) that they miss out on God's amazing love.

Your best friend is dating a guy and rarely has time for you anymore.

Instead of wanting to spend time with you on the weekend, your dad is content to veg on the couch, remote control in one hand and a bag of chips in the other.

You find out on Monday morning that your friends went to the mall and the movies over the weekend and didn't invite you.

These experiences are painful, and they bring up some great questions (see ASK YOURSELF.) Those responses are perfectly normal. God designed you to crave relationships. The love of other people is supposed to give you a taste of God's love. Here's the bad news: many girls get so distracted by boys, their dads, their friends, or other stuff (like money, clothes, and sports) that they miss out on God's amazing love.

ASK YOURSELF:
>IF GOD IS WILD ABOUT ME, AND HE IS SUPPOSED TO MEET THE NEEDS OF MY LIFE, THEN WHY DO I DESPERATELY WANT A BOYFRIEND?
>WHY DO I GET MY FEELINGS HURT WHEN MY DAD IGNORES ME?
>WHY DO I WANT TO CRY WHEN A FRIEND DOESN'T INVITE ME TO HER PARTY?

"I JUST WANT TO FEEL LOVED!"

Made for Him

When God created you, He made you for Himself. He wants a special relationship with you, so He created you uniquely.

Check out Genesis 1:26-27 below to see how you've been created uniquely. But to read this Scripture passage, you'll need to hold it up to a mirror.

"Let Us make man in Our image, according to Our likeness. They will rule the fish of the sea, the birds of the sky, the animals, all the earth, and the creatures that crawl on the earth." So God created man in His own image; He created him in the image of God; He created them male and female.
—Genesis 1:26-27

How did the mirror help you read these verses? The mirror reflected an image. Just like a mirror reflects what's in front of it, you are a reflection of your Creator. That's what it means to be created *in His image*. You reflect a bit of who God is.

One way you reflect Him is your need for relationships. You were created to want relationships, primarily a relationship with the One who made you. And that's why a relationship with God is so important for your life.

In *The Message*, Eugene Peterson paraphrased Ephesians 1:4-5 like this:

✳ GOD MADE YOU

Where you see a blank line, insert your name.

Long before he laid down earth's foundations, he had _____ in mind, had settled on _____ as the focus of his love, to be made whole and holy by his love. Long, long ago he decided to adopt _____ into his family through Jesus Christ. (What pleasure he took in planning this!) He wanted _____ to enter into the celebration of his lavish gift-giving by the hand of his beloved Son.

The part of you that aches to be filled is your soul, and your soul was made for God!

That Guy

He walks the halls of your school every day, and he attracts the attention of all the girls. The hair. The smile. The muscle. And when he comes near, your knees feel like Jell-O® and you talk like you have peanut butter stuck to the roof of your mouth. When he pays attention to you, your heart feels like it's ready to explode!

Who's the guy who has captured your heart recently? What's his name? What do you like about him?

God designed you to be attracted to guys. It's absolutely normal for you to melt when "that guy" comes around. But keep this truth close to your heart:

> *That gorgeous guy may be hott and funny and strong, but even if he asked you for a date this weekend and every weekend for the next year, he would never—not in a million years—be enough to fill your soul.*

He will never make you whole. He wasn't designed to fill the depth of your longing, to anticipate your every need, and to jump through every hoop. He can't. Those places inside you are reserved for God.

In the Right Place

Want to learn the balance God intends for you to have in your relationship with "that guy"?

Use the following words to fill in the blanks in the paragraph below: beautiful, God, healthy, wild about me, Savior, perfect, opinions.

A healthy relationship with a guy who loves God gives me a glimpse of a part of the love that God has for me. A guy is not _____, and never will be. He is not my _____. He is not the answer to all my dreams and longings. I must learn the difference between guys who are _____ emotionally and spiritually, and guys who are not. And this is critical: I must not mistake his _____ for the opinions of _____. That guy may never call me gorgeous or smart or witty. That doesn't change the fact that I am _____ and smart and funny and amazing. No matter what a guy says or doesn't say, God is still _____!

(Answers: perfect, Savior, healthy, opinions, God, beautiful, wild about me)

God's love gives you wisdom to know whether that guy is good for you, whether he really has your best interests in mind. God's love gives you guidance and patience and hope. A good guy can be wonderful; but he can never be enough, and he can never make you whole. You were made for even more. You were made for God.

If you want to ruin a friendship, expect your best friend to make you happy.

Your Other Father

Remember the mirror illustration? You know how you reflect part of God's character because you're created in His image? That same principle applies to a special person in your life—your dad. As your earthly father, your dad

is supposed to mirror God's character and God's love.

If your dad never calls you beautiful, if he never asks you to dance, if his words or his hands wound you, then you haven't seen a picture of God's love. And because of that personal loss, you may have a hard time understanding God's love for you.

It's OK to hesitate and to question. You have good reason. But you must not let your earthly father (or lack of one) drive you away from God's perfect love.

Your Friends

Check all the things you do with your friends:

- [ ] play sports
- [ ] hang out
- [ ] go to church
- [ ] talk about guys
- [ ] shop
- [ ] blow off steam
- [ ] do service projects
- [ ] listen to each other
- [ ] pray together
- [ ] do homework
- [ ] instant message
- [ ] listen to music
- [ ] watch movies
- [ ] go out to eat

Friends are awesome, but they can never meet your needs the way God can. If you want to ruin a friendship, expect your best friend to make you happy. Count on her to fix your problems. In the end, she'd feel pressure. She'd disappoint you. You two would grow distant. All the time and work it took to build a friendship would be blown to pieces. Sure, she's amazing; but she cannot be enough. That place is reserved for God.

An Instant "I Love You"

Sometimes God uses the arms of a guy to hold you. Sometimes He calls on the strength of a father to shape you. Sometimes He sends you an instant "I love you" through the cell phone of your best friend. All of these loves are blessings God gives you. Think of them as appetizers intended to make you want more. You have been given an invitation to indulge in the feast of God's love. Don't settle for less. Remember, God thinks you're gorgeous! He is swept away by your beauty. He has given you other loves as gifts, but He's the only Love who can fill your soul. He's the only One who will ever be enough. His love will make you whole. Who would want to miss a love like that?✿

✳ THE GOOD FATHER

Insert your name in the following spaces.

It may be tough, but I, _____, believe that God is not distant. He is not judgmental toward _____. He does not reject _____.
He will never harm _____. He is a good Father who wants good things for _____.
He loves _____ perfectly.

"Right now, I just
want to jump and dance.
Now I realize God loves me
and has always loved me
just the way I am."

Dance

Celebrate His Love

More Mean Girl

(continued from page 14)

The reason most mean girls are mean is they long for love and acceptance. They want everybody else to feel low because they're at their lowest. They don't like themselves.

Back then I had no problem getting in a girl's face about something. If the girls in my clique knew we had succeeded in upsetting someone, then that girl was an easy target and we'd say, "Oh, let's do that again!"

I don't know why, but hurting others made us feel better. What most people didn't know was that we looked like we had it all together, but inside we were hurting, too. And we were afraid others might laugh at us, so we would laugh first. Back then I wore many masks because I was so scared to be myself. I was scared people wouldn't like me and that I wouldn't be accepted.

It was at a youth retreat that God really got through to me. We had a guest speaker, and he happened to be my friend Jenny's youth minister. He was talking about Jenny and her life. Jenny wasn't there because she had killed herself a year earlier.

Jenny had a tough home life. Her dad was abusive, and finally her mom left him. But after that, her mom had a boyfriend and got pregnant. Then her mom was diagnosed with cancer. She couldn't have treatments because they would hurt the baby.

THE REST OF MY STORY

So basically, she had to sit there and let the cancer grow for nine months.

During that time, Jenny was uncool in the eyes of my clique. A good friend would have stuck by her, but I didn't. I avoided her. Her mom died about a month after the baby was born.

I actually talked to Jenny the night before she killed herself, and she was like, "Can you do me a favor? Will you call me in the morning?" And I said, "Sure." But I didn't call her.

In second period they told us that Jenny had killed herself. I immediately thought, *She never would have killed herself if I had called her and been there for her all those months.*

At the retreat, Jenny's youth minister talked about Jenny and about blame. He talked about how we treat others badly and how we need to take off our masks and be ourselves with people. I completely broke down. That was my turning point.

Jenny's youth minister helped me recognize who I am in Christ—that I am a child of God. He created me and is wild about me. But He didn't create me to be a mean girl or to act like I was better than everybody else. And He certainly wasn't pleased with my behavior. But He has forgiven me. And now every day I want to be a beautiful reflection of Him.

I don't have to wear masks anymore; God loves me just as I am. My prayer is that you, too, will come to understand just how much God loves you. You don't have

> "She never would have killed herself if I had called her and been there for her all those months."

to wear masks anymore either! Be yourself because God loves you inside and out!

When I finally became comfortable with myself, I realized that if someone doesn't like me for who I am, then I don't need that person as a friend. No one does.

I wish I had learned these truths sooner. I wish I had been there for Jenny. Each day I pray that I can somehow shatter the distorted mirrors girls use to see themselves and others. I want girls to see God's love reflected in me. I want them to see themselves through His eyes so they can know just how beautiful they really are. ✻

VIEW

How did the last guy you dated make you feel?

left behind

"I dated this guy, and he would always go back to his old girlfriend. It was hard to accept second place." —Amanda, 18

emotionally abused

"I've been in an emotionally and physically abusive relationship. It's very hard to get out. I would rather be hit in the face a thousand times than be hit with words." —Kristin, 17

disrespected

"My last relationship was horrible. I remember he would yell at me for no reason. I always did everything wrong, according to him. Finally, I was like, 'not anymore,' and I ended it." —Sarah, 16

instant message

God is the only Love who can fill your soul. He is the only One who will ever be enough. His love promises to make you whole.

Who would want to miss a love like that?

appreciated

"I recently met this guy. When he saw me for the first time, he said, 'Hey, beautiful!' When he said that I knew I wanted to be with him. I need that person to tell me that I'm beautiful." —Becca, 16

innergirl

Ask Angela

home alone

Q It seems like I am the only one of my friends without a boyfriend. I try to be happy for them, but on the inside it makes me feel sad and lonely. What can I do?

A I hear you. I didn't really have a boyfriend until I was in college. In high school, it felt like all my girlfriends were going out on dates while I was sitting at home. Here are the best things God has taught me about waiting through those years.

First, take your loneliness to God. Be honest with Him. Tell Him your desires. Ask Him to comfort your soul give you peace in your heart. Our God is a compassionate God. He will hear you and respond with great love.

Next, spend your extra time becoming someone amazing. Don't just sit around in front of the TV feeling sorry for yourself. Make plans with friends. Exercise. Play sports. Do something crafty. Give away your time to help other people. Spend time with God. When you decide to use your time positively, you'll become a very interesting and captivating grown-up woman who is more prepared for a relationship. You can discover what you like and who you want to spend time with.

And last, don't go out with someone just because you're lonely or everyone else has someone. Choose wisely.

> Don't just sit around in front of the TV feeling sorry for yourself. Make plans with friends. Exercise. Play sports. Do something crafty. Give away your time to help other people. Spend time with God.

no future

Q I've been disappointed by friends and some people in my family. School has been hard. I don't have much hope that the future will be any better. What do you think?

A I have the absolute best news ever: the God of hope is wild about you! He wants to give you a future beyond what you can dream for yourself (Eph. 3:20).

Life is hard. We are imperfect and so is our world. But God is coming through all the time. Sometimes He waits for you to be ready to receive His blessings. But sometimes, your whole life can change for good in a moment. Here's your responsibility:

1. Keep a strong relationship with God. Depend on Him. Pray to Him. Learn about Him.

2. Believe that He is the God of your future, even if you can't see how it's all going to work out. Our hope comes in the unseen (Rom. 8:24).

3. Ask God to take away your fears and give you courage—courage to dream big dreams and trust God for the impossible. Keep your head up and believe God when He promises to give you hope.

Angela Thomas is crazy about her four teenage and preteen kids. She is a great carpool driver, baseball watcher, and flat-iron stylist. When the kids can't think of anything else for her to do, she writes books for women and speaks at events around the country. www.angelathomas.com

God, I don't
hate You. I just
don't know how
to love You. Or
why you would
love me.

Love on the Line

Dear God,

My student minister says You're my Heavenly Father. He says You'll care for me like earthly fathers who love and take care of their children. But that scares me. I guess that's why I'm writing You this letter. It's easier for me to talk to You this way. I want to love You and trust You, but I'm afraid of You.

My dad isn't like other dads. He doesn't go to my ball games or ask me about my life. He still doesn't know that Aaron and I broke up, and that was three weeks ago. He has never told me I'm beautiful. He doesn't really talk to me, except when I make bad grades or get in fights with Mom. He reminds me about all the mistakes I've made and tells me I'll never amount to anything. I'm a disappointment to him. I wish I could make him happy, maybe then he would love me and want to be with me.

Can I be honest with You, God? If you're like my dad, I don't want to know You. I don't want to disappoint You. And I'm really scared of You. I don't want You to punish me when I mess up, which is all the time. (Sorry about cheating on that test, by the way.) Most of all, I'm afraid You'll hurt me. I'm afraid You won't really love me and won't be there for me when it hurts, like when Aaron started dating Britney.

God, I don't hate You. I just don't know how to love You. Or why You would love me. Can You help me? Will You still love me even though I don't know how to love You? I want to get close to You but I don't know how.

—Nikki

> *You are My child, and I will not wound your tender heart.... I'll never turn you away. Come to Me, and I'll pick you up and hold you against My heart. Always.*

My Precious Nikki,

My love for you will never be determined by whether or not you love Me. I loved you before you were born, and My love is constant—even when you can't see it or feel it. I know your heart. I know you love Me as best as you can.

Think about it this way: if a toddler waddles up to a father and mumbles something while reaching to be picked up, will that father scold her because she didn't know how to ask to be held? Will that father refuse to hold his baby because she didn't know how to form the words, "I love you, Daddy"? Of course not.

You are My child, and I will not wound your tender heart. I love that you're willing to come to Me with your cries of honesty. I'll never turn you away. I'll pick you up and hold you against My heart. Always.

A relationship with Me is a lot like your friendship with Katie. You were leery of her at first, but the more you got to know her, the more you liked her.

Trusting Me is like that. You have lots of assumptions about who I am and what I'm like. You see Me as an absent, distant Father who is disappointed in you and can't wait to punish you for making mistakes. But keep trying to get to know Me, and you'll discover that your assumptions about Me are all wrong. I'm not absent. I'm not distant. And I'm certainly not disappointed in you. I'm a perfect, loving Father who is wild about you! The more time we spend together, the more you'll learn to trust Me. Just keep seeking Me, even when you're scared. You'll find in Me a love that won't ever let you go.

—Love, God

7days

My World

1 girl's week off

Take a boy break this week. Spend that time with God.

✻ Things to do this week to remind yourself God's love will fill your soul.

the message

2 Make a color poster of the following and mount it on the ceiling above your bed.

God is the only Love who can fill my soul. He is the only One who will ever be enough. His love promises to make me whole. I don't want to miss a love like that!

friend or foe?

3 Ask yourself which of your friends have a positive influence on your life and which have a negative influence.

pray every day

4 Pray every day this week for God to bring a positive male role model into your life.

pop rocks!

5 If you have an attentive father, thank God for him and tell your dad how much he means to you.

honor your hero

Ask your dad for a date.

6

give good vibes

Make a positive influence on another girl this week.

7

In My Own Words

The traits I want in a boyfriend are

When I'm around my dad he makes me feel

When I'm around my boyfriend he makes me feel

When I'm around my best friend she makes me feel

If I were totally convinced God thinks I'm gorgeous and loves me even when my breath is bad and my hair looks gross, I would

Set your spirit free.

soar
find real freedom in christ

Whispers of Unbelief

"Why am I so afraid that I don't measure up and never will?"

Voices in My Head

WHY AM I SO AFRAID THAT I DON'T MEASURE UP AND NEVER WILL?

by Angela Thomas

GORGEOUS. God, I'm struggling here. I believe that You said it, but did You really mean it about me? Good grief. You see me in the shower for heaven's sake! *Gorgeous* is not the first word that would pop into my head. *Average* might be the word I'd use. *Common. Ordinary.* But not GORGEOUS!

If anyone knows the truth about this body, it's You. Every jiggle and wiggle. You witness my attempts to suck it all in. You see me first thing in the morning every single day. And beyond my body, there is my heart. Again, gorgeous doesn't really come to mind here either. *Flawed. Inconsistent. Petty. Insecure.* All those words seem to speak the truth that hides inside me.

How could You call me gorgeous?

Are You sure? I know You are God, and of course You're sure; but maybe You had some poetic imagery in mind. Maybe You were speaking in broad terms about the beauty of Your creation. Did You really think of me when You said, "The king is enthralled with your beauty"? The King is wild about me?

I keep hearing these voices in my head: "Don't believe it, don't believe all of it. It's too good to be true." It could be like the guy who said I was gorgeous but forgot to call me. He only meant it in the moment, not for real.

BELIEVING. It seems to be the key to the whole deal with You. I desperately want to believe, but unbelief interrupts my effort. Doubts come to me. Skepticism speaks to me. Sometimes I hear what others haven't said about me more loudly than I can hear You.

I believe in You, so why does unbelief still whisper to me? Why am I prone to incline my head and listen?

Why am I so afraid that I don't measure up and never will? ✽

Pop Quiz

What do you fear the most? Not fitting in? Looking stupid? Or are you afraid that God doesn't really love you? Take this quiz to find out which worries hold you back the most. Read each statement in all six categories. Think about how you would feel in each situation. Score each one with a 0–3 based on this scale:

0 = I don't really worry too much about this.
1 = I sometimes worry about this.
2 = I worry about this a lot.
3 = This is one of my biggest fears.

A. Fitting In

- [ ] My first day at a new school
- [ ] Being in a situation where I don't know anyone
- [ ] Not being included in what my friends are doing
- [ ] Feeling different from everyone else
- [ ] Wanting to be part of the popular crowd

B. Not Measuring Up

- [ ] Making good grades
- [ ] Feeling like I don't have the same privileges as my friends
- [ ] Being good at whatever I do (sports, work, hobbies)
- [ ] Not having as much money as my friends
- [ ] Having the right clothes, car, cell phone, etc.

C. Looking Stupid

- [ ] Speaking or performing in front of an audience
- [ ] Tripping in the hall at school
- [ ] Having people laugh at me
- [ ] Being caught wearing something others would make fun of
- [ ] A teacher calling on me when I don't know the answer

D. Not Being Loved

- [ ] Getting dumped by my boyfriend
- [ ] Having a fight with my best friend and not making up
- [ ] Being criticized by people
- [ ] Never finding my "soul mate"
- [ ] Getting my feelings hurt by someone I care about

E. Messing up My Life

- [ ] Not getting into the right college
- [ ] Failing an important test or class
- [ ] Coming in second place in anything
- [ ] Disappointing my friends or family in a big way
- [ ] Getting into trouble and not knowing a way out

F. God Doesn't Really Love Me

- [ ] Feeling like I've made too many mistakes
- [ ] Not knowing for sure if I'm really saved
- [ ] Wondering if God really listens to me
- [ ] Thinking I may have committed an unforgivable sin
- [ ] Wondering if I do enough good stuff to please God

Scoring: Add your score for each section separately. The group with the highest number is your biggest fear. Read the explanations below to find out what this means for you.

A. It sounds like you're really concerned about fitting in. Being consumed with it can make a person more likely to cave in to peer pressure in order to be liked. Try to learn ways to be more confident in your uniqueness and independence. Get some advice from your mentor or student minister and know that God strengthens and rewards us when we try to please Him above others.

B. Wondering how you measure up to others is a big fear for you. You struggle with feeling like you have to do all the right things or have all the right stuff to be liked. But when you're so focused on your own situation, it's hard to see reality. Step back and evaluate what you do have, what you are good at, and relax!

C. Who doesn't worry about looking stupid or being caught in an embarrassing situation? Next time you flub your speech or trip up the steps, laugh it off and move on. Chances are, people will remember your sense of humor and grace more than your mistake. They'll think, *Wow! She's so confident and relaxed!*

D. Does "looking for love in all the wrong places" sound familiar? Maybe you feel insecure with some of your relationships, or you are overly sensitive to criticism. These attitudes can lead you to make some big mistakes when you try too hard to get approval. Everyone needs to be loved, but only God can love you unconditionally, perfectly, and completely. Seek that kind of love from Him and you will be satisfied.

E. It sounds as if you fear really messing up your life. It's great that you care so much about important things like family, friends, and being successful. This desire, if you focus it in the right way, can take you far in life. But girl, no human is perfect! Putting so much pressure on yourself only makes you feel worse, right? You can be so focused on not making mistakes that you end up with a messed up perspective on life. Jesus said for us to seek Him first, then the rest will fall into place. (See Matt. 6:33.) Do this and you will succeed.

F. Are you afraid God doesn't really love you? You're not alone in this fear, but it seems to have taken a pretty strong hold on you. If you've asked God's forgiveness, you're forgiven, rest assured! Speak with a counselor, pastor, your Bible study leader, or a Christian friend about these worries. When you get this one settled in your heart, you can face any other fears with faith.

Deeper

SCREAM!!

Unchecked, fear can take over your life.

L ots of people fear stuff. Some fears, or phobias as they're also called, are more common than others. Match the phobias on the left with the correct definition on the right.

□ 1. Alektorophobia   a. The fear of otters
□ 2. Chionophobia   b. The fear of chins
□ 3. Sciophobia   c. The fear of chickens
□ 4. Geniophobia   d. The fear of snow
□ 5. Lutraphobia   e. The fear of shadows

(Answers: 1. c; 2. d; 3. e; 4. b; 5. a)

Do you ever ask yourself, "What if they don't like me?" or "What if I look stupid?" Those questions are steeped in fear.

While some of these phobias may seem silly to you, they have a crippling effect on others. The truth about fear is this: left unchecked, it can take over your life. It can whisper into your soul like a quiet disease and can leave you spiritually crippled and paralyzed.

The Sound of Fear

Fear can rob you of the truth about yourself and lead you to think that you can't possibly be beautiful, especially to God. Fear sounds like this:

There's no way God can really love me. I've messed up too much.

or

I'll never be good enough.

Do you ever ask yourself, "What if they don't like me?" or "What if I look stupid?" Those questions are steeped in fear—fear of not fitting in, measuring up, or being loved; fear of looking stupid and messing up; and fear of being unworthy of God's affection.

Where do these fears about yourself come from? Usually they are formed over time and are shaped by different factors. Below are self-image scenarios that may trip your memory about your own fears.

The world has made you fear that you will never, ever measure up to its standards, but you better try hard anyway!

"WHY CAN'T THEY JUST LEAVE ME ALONE?"

ASK YOURSELF:
> DO I FEAR LOOKING STUPID TO KIDS AT SCHOOL?
> DO I BEAT MYSELF UP WHEN I MAKE A MISTAKE?
> DO I FIND IT DIFFICULT TO FORGIVE MYSELF?
> DO I FEAR THAT I NEVER WILL BE GOOD ENOUGH?

After being hit with the world's messages every day, how could you not buy into them? Essentially, you've been brainwashed by the world. The world has made you fear that you'll never, ever measure up to its standards, but you better try hard anyway!

✳ SELF-IMAGE WORST-CASE SCENARIO

List some things that have shaped the way you see yourself. Use the cues on the right to help you fill in the blanks.

1 _____ (describe a grade-school or junior high taunting)
2 _____ (recall hateful words spoken by someone)
3 _____ (recall an embarrassing moment in the hallway at school)
4 _____ (list a magazine's image of beauty)
5 _____ (name a movie's expectation of value)
6 _____ (list an unattainable beauty tip)
7 _____ (recall a bad mistake you just can't forget)

Combat Fear

So how do you combat the fear? You have a choice: you can choose to listen to the fear and let it dictate what you think about yourself, or you can choose to listen to what God says about you.

✳ COMBATING FEAR

Following are common issues teen girls struggle with. For each one, read the Scripture provided. Write down what that passage says about combating that fear.

"God can't really love me." Romans 8:38-39

"I'm not special." Psalm 139:13-16

"I'm afraid of rejection." Galatians 1:10

"I can't measure up." Colossians 1:21-22

Live the Belief

Maybe no one in this world has ever called you beautiful. Maybe you've made lots of mistakes. Maybe you have been embarrassed, shamed, or ridiculed—and that has left you feeling unloved, unwanted, or unworthy. To believe that you are valued, loved, and beautiful is just too unbelievable.

But here's the really big deal: you look into the mirror with YOUR eyes. That's the problem. God doesn't see as you see (or as the world sees). He sees through perfect eyes and He sees you as beautiful all the way around.

You look into the mirror with YOUR eyes. That's the problem.

What if you began to live as if you believed God thinks you're gorgeous and He is wild about you? What if you lived by faith instead of fear? What if you traded what you feel about yourself for the truth of His words? Do you have anything to lose? No. And to gain? The rest of your life resting in the arms of God, secure in a love that makes life a glorious adventure! ✻

In the space below, write a note to God, committing to trust the truth of His words instead of your fear. If fears still have a grip on your heart, ask Him to help you overcome them.

LIVE
the
Belief

It's A Glorious Adventure

VIEW

How do you fight the fear of not measuring up?

Bible & friends encourage me

get real

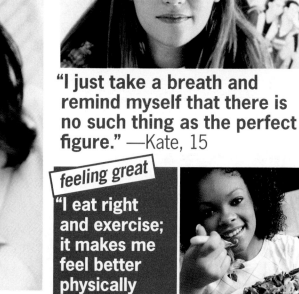

"I just take a breath and remind myself that there is no such thing as the perfect figure." —Kate, 15

feeling great

"I eat right and exercise; it makes me feel better physically and mentally." —Monique, 19

"I go to the Word, especially when I'm getting down on myself. And I go to good friends who encourage me." —Carleigh, 16

mentored

"I have a good role model that I can look up to for inner and outer beauty." —Ellen, 14

✳ instant message

God's love, grace, and mercy are greater than your mistakes, doubts, and fears.

Ask Angela

running out

Angela, you say that you can never use up all of God's love, but you don't know what I've done. I can't forgive myself for what I've done, so how can God forgive me?

Sometimes we can begin thinking God is like us. Our love is fickle. We can forgive a friend a few times, but then later decide not to. We act and respond in our humanity. But God is not like us. He is divine.

Think about this. Did you wake up this morning and turn on the radio to hear that there were air supply rations in your city? Did a reporter say that everyone should refrain from taking a deep breath today because we have almost reached our air quota for the year? Sounds silly doesn't it? We all know that the air doesn't run out. It is replenished every day. We don't have to worry about having enough air to breathe.

It's the same with God's love. You cannot use up all His forgiveness. You did not receive only a portion of grace that is supposed to last you a lifetime. His forgiveness is not limited to "little sin."

Maybe you think that you cannot be forgiven. But God forgives with His great, big, divine love. That's why we get down on our knees and cry, "Holy!" When God has forgiven you much, your gratefulness wants to worship Him and tell everyone about His amazing love!

> You cannot use up all His forgiveness. You did not receive only a portion of grace that is supposed to last you a lifetime. His forgiveness is not limited to "little sin."

voices in my head

I don't think I know how to hear God's voice. I only hear stuff in my head and sometimes I don't know if it's God or Satan. Can you help me?

Satan is the enemy and he tells you lies to distract you from hearing God's voice. Below are three ways to know if you are hearing from the Accuser (Satan) instead of God.

First, Satan always spotlights sin, even sin that has been forgiven and covered by the grace of God. He will keep reminding you of your sin as long as you will listen.

Second, the Accuser brings confusion. He plants weeds in your heart, hoping to choke out all the good work God is doing.

Third, Satan wants to be louder than the truth. He will keep telling lies until you are wounded. God is a healer. He wants to replace the lies with truth and heal your broken heart.

When I was learning to hear God's voice, I spent time with people who knew God. I'd tell them what I was thinking and ask, "Does that sound like God?" They helped me figure out whom I was hearing.

Angela Thomas is crazy about her four teenage and preteen kids. She is a great carpool driver, baseball watcher, and flat-iron stylist. When the kids can't think of anything else for her to do, she writes books for women and speaks at events around the country. www.angelathomas.com

Cutting It Close

An interview with Sara Acker of the band Inhabited

my mission

Q: It's obvious that you have a real heart for teenage girls. How did that come about?

A: When I was 12, I saw this TV show about Russia. Teenage girls were interviewed, and their only aspiration was to become prostitutes. That was their dream! That's when it hit me. Even though I was young and still had growing to do on my own, I sensed a passion to reach girls.

backstage

Q: After a concert, how do you continue your message to girls?

A: Shows can be kinda crazy afterwards, signing autographs and everything. But someone always comes up broken or needing prayer, and I've been able to spend time with them. E-mail also has been a really big thing for me—corresponding with girls about all the things they're going through.

vital connections

Q: Why do you think girls open up to you more than their parents or closest friends?

A: If you're writing an e-mail, you feel like you can totally pour out your heart. I remember one girl wrote, "I'm so sick of it, because people think I'm just this Jesus Freak, but I'm dying on the inside." It was her way of expressing what she was feeling, even though everyone around her thought everything was perfect in her life. She could really be honest through e-mail. She wasn't going to be judged. As a band, we really try to show love. Our song "If We Could Love (we could change the world)" has that perspective.

biggest struggle

Q: What do you believe is the biggest struggle teenage girls face?

A: Beauty and outward appearance. There's so much emphasis on that. Society had idolized beauty—the more beautiful you are externally, the better celebrity you are. Nothing is based on character. We're constantly bombarded with images of what we're supposed to be like, and that's a battle. Realizing that my worth is not found in external beauty but in the pursuit of character has been a personal journey for me.

media bias

Q: How do you personally battle the influence of the media?

A: I shut certain entertainment doors. I don't read certain maga-zines or watch certain shows, because if you constantly fill your my mind with that stuff, it's definitely going to influence you. Society makes it look like a killer body equals worth. And if you're constantly putting those images in your brain, it's going to be very hard not to pursue the whole vanity thing. I've learned that when I'm focused on myself, that's when I'm most conscious of all these things. Whenever I say, "This is who God made me to be," and I look to Him and surrender to Him, it's liberating.

seeing the scars

Q: In one of your songs you reference a girl who cuts herself. Why do you think girls choose such a violent outlet for their emotional pain?

A: The song "One More Night" alludes to this, but the dedication reads, "This is dedicated to those whose scars are hidden and to those whose scars are visible." A lot of times girls cut themselves so that people will see it and recognize the cry, "Hey! This is how deeply I'm hurting! Please take notice of me!" Then there are other girls who hide cutting, and I think that a lot of times they think it's just their way to feel alive. It goes back to being consumed with your situation. You have to find your worth in God. You can either be a God-pleaser or a man-pleaser. ✽

> "This is dedicated to those whose scars are hidden and to those whose scars are visible."

Check out the Inhabited Web site (www.inhabitedtheband.com) to hear their hit CD THE REVOLUTION (Fervent Records). Send e-mails to: Sara@inhabitedtheband.com.

The Jerk

"He didn't have to be so mean," Chelsea said, wiping tears from her face.

by S. Moen

You're such a dork, Chelsea! You make me sick. Nobody likes you!" Chelsea's lip trembled. She clutched her books tighter to her chest as Daniel leaned in and sneered, "Can't take the truth, huh? Go run off to your stupid friends and cry, you big baby!" Daniel's friends snickered as Chelsea dashed down the hall.

In that instant she hated Daniel. She barely made it to the rest room before she burst into tears. Annie saw Chelsea dart in and followed her.

"What happened?"

"Daniel just humiliated me in front of everyone. I hate him!"

"Chelsea, you know Daniel is a jerk. He doesn't care about anyone but himself. But I know something else. He's really afraid. He just acts tough because he doesn't want anyone to know how scared he is that he won't fit in."

Chelsea looked surprised.

"How do you know that?"

"My brother knows him from the basketball team. He says Daniel is really afraid of being an outsider."

"He didn't have to be so mean," Chelsea said, wiping tears from her face.

"Chelsea, what if I told you there is someone who will never hurt you like Daniel did?"

"Right. That'll never happen for me."

"Listen, Chels. I used to feel the same way you do. But I learned something at church that made all the difference. I learned God loves me just as I am, and what He thinks counts more than anybody else."

"Yeah, but you're religious."

"This isn't about being religious. This is about what's true. Trust me."

"OK. So, what does God say?"

"That you are really special to Him. And the reason Jesus came to die on the cross was because God's love for you and me is so great. My student minister says that God searches all over the earth to find the ones who are lost and hurting. I remember when I finally got it. I was at camp and suddenly I knew if God really loved me that much, I could trust Him. Then I started reading what He says about people in the Bible, and I discovered He cares about me more than I ever thought anybody could. And I don't mean He only cares about me when I'm good or smart or pretty. God looks at me and says, 'Annie, I think you're awesome! I've got some great plans for you.' "

"Yeah, but you go to church and you're good. You know me. I've done a lot of stupid things."

"That's what's so cool, Chelsea! God doesn't care what you did. He wipes all that stuff away. He just asks you to let Him take over how you live from now on. He knows exactly what you need to have a life that's great. And besides, if He's God, He knows what He's doing, right?"

Chelsea couldn't argue.

"Do you know why guys like Daniel try to hurt people?" Annie asked. "Because they don't know what it means to be loved by someone who will never fail them. God will always love you, Chelsea—even when you mess up. He only wants what's best for you. Daniel might try to make you feel bad, but Daniel is not God."

"You're right," Chelsea answered. "If God loves me that much, then why should I let someone else tell me I'm not good enough?"

"Good question," said Annie. ❀

> **Daniel might try to make you feel bad, but Daniel is not God.**

My World
7days

*Things to do this week to squash the fear in your life.

1 no Fear!

Memorize Mark 9:23-24 and Isaiah 55:8-9. Remember, God is on your side! Believe who He says He is. Believe what He say about you. And believe you can do all things through Him. He is your shield!

2 swap-a-fear

Write a fear you have. Swap it with a friend. Commit to praying every day this week that God will work wonders to overcome your friend's fear. Ask her to do the same for you.

3 ask a pro

Talk with an older teen who has overcome an embarrassing moment at school.

5 I believe

Don't let anyone tell you you're not good enough.

4 the edge

This week do one thing that scares you. Quote Psalm 28:7 to calm your nerves.

6 toes to head

Start with your feet and work your way up, thanking God for each part of your body.

7 talk...plan...conquer

Talk with your mom or a mentor about the thing you fear most. Develop an action plan for overcoming that fear.

innergirl
In My Own Words

The thing I would like to do most if I could
overcome my fear is

One thing that I used to be afraid of but no
longer am is

I think I'm afraid of _____
because _____.

The bravest girl I know is

I have never been afraid to _____
because _____.

If I could sit down and talk face to
face with Jesus about my fears, I
would tell Him

What Lies Do I Believe?

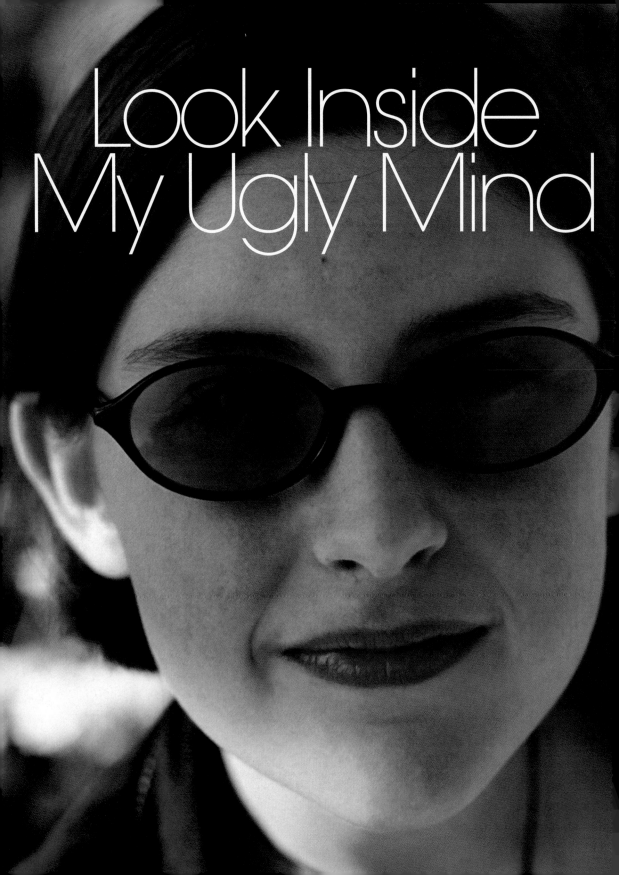

Look Inside
My Ugly Mind

by Emily Cole

LOOKING BACK AT MY TEEN YEARS, I wish I could have seen that my legs weren't ugly. It seems like a silly struggle, but I spent hours critiquing just about every inch of me. What began as an issue with my legs soon led to discontentment with my stomach (it wasn't flat enough), my breasts (not big enough), my skin (not clear enough), my clothes (not trendy enough), and my hair (not straight enough). I spent a lot of time focused on how different I was from the girls I wanted to be like.

> It's really not fair that girls in our society are held to a standard of "perfection" that can't be attained without the help of a computer, a makeup artist, or a plastic surgeon.

A Distorted View

I now believe I suffered from a distorted view of my own body, planted in my mind by Satan to keep me discouraged and self-conscious. I wanted a different body—a perfect body; and I wasn't the only one. Most of my friends had body image issues too, even the girls I envied! In this sick chain of earthly role models Satan has established, there will always be discontentment. Admiring someone for what they look like or what they have will only leave you empty. I know—I've been there.

It's No Wonder

Of course, it didn't help that the media was blasting me every step of the way with images of the so-called perfect body—skinny. It's no wonder we're all confused.

My body is a gift from God. He created it the way He did for a reason. And I'm grateful for His gift.

"IT'S NOT FAIR!"

It's no wonder so many of us have eating disorders. We see all these images on TV and in magazines of people with pretty faces, perfect makeup, and bodies that are nothing more than skin and bones, except in certain areas where they've been "enhanced."

If I look like the girl in the magazine then everyone will like me, we think to ourselves. But we don't realize the hours of preparation that go into every image presented to us by the media to create the image of perfection that we see. Magazines retouch the pictures of the celebrities they feature. Movie stars employ stylists to make them look their best. It's really not fair that girls in our society are held to an unrealistic standard of perfection that can't be attained without the assistance of a computer, a makeup artist, or a plastic surgeon.

It wasn't until I went to college that I realized I don't have to be like everyone else. Unlike high school, which can be so cutthroat and superficial, college is a place where people are less afraid to be themselves. The independence to be whomever God created you to be is nurtured on the college campus.

I think it's heartbreaking that Satan uses the earthly home for our souls against us in an effort to starve us spiritually. I still struggle from time to time with not liking my body. But I've decided that instead of focusing on what my legs are not, I will focus on what they are: healthy, strong, and capable of getting me anywhere I need to go. My body is a gift from God. He created it the way He did for a reason. And I'm grateful for His gift.❋

ASK YOURSELF:

> DO I BELIEVE I HAVE TO BE SKINNY TO BE PRETTY?
> DO I FEEL SUB-ZERO IF I CAN'T BUY THE LATEST FASHION?
> DO I BELIEVE THAT IF I LOOK LIKE THE GIRL IN THE MAGAZINE EVERYONE WILL LIKE ME?
> AM I AFRAID TO BE MYSELF?

"When you see ads of sexy, swanky girls tossing their hair for a shampoo commercial, that image sticks. You may not think anything of it while you're watching TV, but it changes the way you think."
—Cynthia, 16

"Perfect celebrity bodies and models are everywhere. But none of those images is true; they have all been airbrushed and fixed on a computer to show a perfect body that doesn't even exist. Girls see these images and they try to aspire to something that isn't real. Every day I see pictures of beautiful, perfect women and I think, *I have to look like that!* And every day I have to remind myself that nobody really looks like that."
—Tasha, 21

"I've decided to stop watching commercials with 'sexy' girls—especially those shampoo commercials. That has helped. I'm not through yet, but the problem is fixing itself. Satan really knows how to sneak in. You have to learn to sneak him out!" —Hannah, 14

"Magazine pictures are always touched up. All they put in there are the perfect girls who look like Barbie® dolls."
—Rachel Ann, 16

WHAT'S EATING YOU?

"In sixth grade I made myself throw up a lot. Girls think that not eating is the one thing they can control that their parents can't."
—Caitlin, 17

"The biggest pressures girls face are boys, clothes, and the way we look." —Leah, 14

"I used to have an eating disorder in seventh and eighth grades. There was this guy I liked and I was starving myself for him. I had to be perfect. I kept thinking I was the fattest thing ever, but I wasn't." —Shelby, 16

Quiz 1

Disordered Eating Checklist

Instructions: Check the boxes next to the statements that are true for you.

☐ 1. I'm always on some kind of diet.
☐ 2. I sometimes eat too much when I get stressed, worried, lonely, mad—you name it!
☐ 3. I worry about getting fat.
☐ 4. I'm a real pro when it comes to counting calories, fat grams, carbs, and all that stuff.
☐ 5. I skip meals when I need to lose weight.
☐ 6. I'm unhappy with the way my body looks.
☐ 7. I have made myself throw up (or used something to make me go to the bathroom) when I wasn't sick.
☐ 8. If someone tells me my body looks good, I know they must be lying! They just don't see what I see.
☐ 9. I'm obsessed with losing weight or making sure I don't gain any.
☐ 10. Sometimes I feel ashamed or guilty after I eat.
☐ 11. Some people might think I exercise too much.
☐ 12. I've been told I'm too skinny.

If you checked 3 or more of these statements, or especially if you answered yes to numbers 7 or 9, please go on to the next quiz now.

If you checked less than 3, great! You probably have pretty normal attitudes about eating and about your body. If you're like most girls, you know it's hard to keep your chin up when everywhere you look the messages are about being pretty or thin, but you're not likely to do anything drastic to yourself. Keep up the good attitude and the healthy lifestyle! Your body will thank you for it.

"I have a friend who wears a size 5, and she's always like 'I need to do situps.' It kills me." —Olivia, 16

Eating Disorders Checklist

Instructions: OK girls, here's where we need to get specific. Check the boxes next to the statements that are true for you. Please be honest—no one will know your answers unless you choose to share them.

- ☐ 1. People tell me (or I know) I'm skinnier than I should be for someone my age.
- ☐ 2. An adult or someone I trust has told me they are concerned about my weight or eating habits.
- ☐ 3. I've missed several periods in a row, even though I'm usually fairly regular.
- ☐ 4. Sometimes I eat way too much at one time.
- ☐ 5. It makes me feel better to be in control over how much (or how little) I eat.
- ☐ 6. I think I see my body differently than everyone else does.
- ☐ 7. I make myself throw up (or use something to make me go to the bathroom) pretty regularly.
- ☐ 8. My biggest fear is getting fat.
- ☐ 9. Sometimes I feel out of control when I eat.
- ☐ 10. My self-esteem is all about how my body looks.
- ☐ 11. I skip meals almost every day to avoid gaining weight.
- ☐ 12. I'm kind of secretive about what I eat or don't eat.
- ☐ 13. I exercise constantly to lose weight or keep from getting fat.

If you didn't check any of these statements, relax! You don't have the symptoms of a true eating disorder. However, some of your attitudes about eating, dieting, and self-esteem could use some tweaking. Eating disorders can develop when people are overwhelmed with the pressure to be thin and don't learn healthier ways of dealing. Talk to someone you trust and check out the Web sites at the end of this quiz to find out more.

If you checked one or more of these statements, you have warning signs of an eating disorder. Don't mess around! Eating disorders are serious business and can be life-threatening. Please, show this quiz to someone you trust (your Bible study leader, a parent, or your doctor), and ask her to help you find a counselor who specializes in eating disorders and can help you feel good about yourself without having to do things that harm your body. Also check out these Web sites: www.anad.org www.nationaleatingdisorders.org www.anred.com

"My friend, a professional model, had an agent who told her she was too big. But she was 5'10" and only weighed 110! She started not eating and made herself sick. But he still thought she was fat. So she fired him and gave it all up. She's happy now." —Rae, 15

"I had to see myself as everyone else saw me: a thin, unhealthy, teenager. I asked God to heal me. My family and friends wanted nothing but for me to be healthy again, which meant not only being a healthy weight but having a healthy mind and the ability to see myself as God made me. I'm not perfect; I wasn't made that way. I like myself a whole lot more now that I understand that." —Whitney, 21

Deeper

Lie Detector

The lies that your culture, the world, and Satan have been telling you will only be silenced by listening to God's voice and believing what He says about you.

Why are people so quick to believe an urban legend? Because the more you hear something, the more you begin to believe it's true. If a little girl is told over and over that she's stupid, she'll begin to believe it.

The same applies to the lies you're told every day. Chances are, you don't even recognize that you're being fed lies because you've heard them for so long. What do they sound like?

"SEXIER ABS IN 10 DAYS!"

"BEAUTY 101: GET YOUR PERFECT LOOK!"

"360 WAYS TO BE IRRESISTIBLE"

"HOW TO MAKE YOUR LIPS ABSOLUTELY PERFECT"

Do these pitches sound familiar? They should; they're actual headlines from magazines. They sound truthful, don't they? If you're careful, though, you can hear the lie underneath: your worth is determined by your physical beauty. And if you're like most girls, you've bought into this lie without question. How do you know if you're living by a lie? Take the Beauty Myths test on page 98.

Where do all the lies come from, ultimately? And why do we believe them? A story from the New Testament will answer those questions.

✳ 10 LIES THE MEDIA TELL YOU EVERY DAY

❶ To be beautiful you must be skinny.
❷ To be beautiful you must wear the lastest fashion.
❸ Only certain clothing brands are hip.
❹ You must look like everyone else to be cool.
❺ Modesty is out of style.
❻ You must dress sexy to attract the attention of guys.
❼ Your value is determined by how you look.
❽ Casual sex is cool.
❾ Abortion is a woman's choice.
❿ Makeup is mandatory.

Read the Scripture below. Draw a big circle around the source of the lies you hear.

Jesus said to them, "If God were your Father, you would love Me, because I came from God and I am here. For I didn't come on My own, but He sent Me. Why don't you understand what I say? Because you cannot listen to My word. You are of your father the Devil, and you want to carry out your father's desires. He was a murderer from the beginning and has not stood in the truth, because there is no truth in him. When he tells a lie, he speaks from his own nature, because he is a liar and the father of liars"
(John 8:42-44).

In this story, Jesus was talking to the Pharisees, who had rejected Him as the Messiah. He explained the nature of lies—they come from Satan.

ASK YOURSELF:
> WHAT'S THE LIE THE MEDIA TELL ME THAT I ALWAYS BELIEVE?
> WHY DO I WANT TO LOOK LIKE THE GIRLS IN THE MAGAZINES I READ?
> WHY AM I SO AFRAID TO DRESS DIFFERENTLY THAN MY FRIENDS?
> WHY AM I SHOWING SO MUCH SKIN?
> DO I BELIEVE MY VALUE IS DETERMINED BY HOW I LOOK?

Think about it. Satan lied to Adam and Eve in the beginning, and he's been lying ever since. He is your enemy—and he wants to destroy your life. (Check out John 10:10 and 1 Peter 5:8.) He uses the culture around you to dominate your thinking, to make you believe you have to look a certain way to be valued. And those lies will dominate your life until you learn to listen to the truth instead. The lies that your culture, the world, and Satan have been telling you will only be silenced by listening to God's voice and believing what He says about you.

Wouldn't it be exciting to believe God instead of the lies you hear from the fashion industry, insensitive family members, movies, even some of your friends? Wouldn't it be great, so freeing, to believe all that matters is the eye of the Beholder? If you believed that, what changes would you make in your daily life? Write those changes here:

Wouldn't it be exciting to believe God instead of the lies you hear from the fashion industry, insensitive family members, movies, even some of your friends?

Now try this exercise. Listed in the sidebar to the right are lies you've probably heard. Take a few minutes, quiet your heart before God, and ask Him to tell you a truth to combat the lies.

The One who calls your name is taken with you. The One who knew you before creation is in love with you. To begin to deal with the lies inside your head is to say, "Hey, I won't listen to this anymore! Get that junk out of my way! I want to hear the truth—the music of love, the love song of my Savior. The Beholder is passionate about me!" ✳

Lie #1: Thinner girls are more attractive than bigger girls. God's Truth:

Lie #2: Guys like me because I show some skin. God's Truth:

Lie #3: When I wear trendy clothes, I'm more attractive. God's Truth:

Lie #4: Being beautiful will take you farther in life. God's Truth:

VIEW

Who's your beauty muse?

neighborhood heros

Jennifer

"Jennifer Garner. She's got muscles!"
—Tatum, 19

God Rules!

"God. He loves me the way I am."
—Amy, 14

"There are these moms in my neighborhood who are Christians. They take good care of their bodies. I look up to them and ask them for advice. They are great role models."
—Jasmine, 19

the perfect girl

"The media have a big say, but I don't listen to them because they're wrong. Instead, I eat healthy and exercise!"
—Mary Catherine, 14

✱ instant message

Satan's lies will only be silenced by listening to God's voice.

innergirl

Ask Angela

dressing sexy?

Q Angela, my boyfriend likes me to dress sexy, and I love the attention I get. What's wrong with that?

A God created you to desire the pleasure of being attractive, but He also made boundaries for your physical and emotional protection. Sexual pleasure is reserved for marriage. Dressing sexy will be a beautiful expression of your love for your husband to be shared in private, within the safety of that commitment.

Your boyfriend is not your husband, so that kind of sexual attention is still inappropriate. You were made to enjoy his attention, but you are still living in the land of "not yet." This is the time to enjoy the attention you get from being funny or intelligent, compassionate or loving. Or maybe you two can enjoy sports or movies. There are a million other things to share and build a relationship on. Now is the time to pursue those.

Enjoying sexual attention is still to come. It's just one of the many pleasures you have to look forward to in marriage. Until marriage, dress with your focus on yourself and your relationship with God. To save "sexy" until marriage is to respect yourself. You can't waste your beautiful on every guy who comes along. Store up this desire to be unveiled in marriage. Save the gift of your sexual attraction for the one who will love you forever.

> God wired us to long for beautiful. He would not wire us for beautiful and then require us to pursue plain. So dress with integrity, but have as much fun as possible!

wired for beauty

Q Some people say that trying to look good (like wearing nice clothes and makeup) is wrong. Can I try to be pretty and still follow God?

A OK, here's where I don't want to contradict anything your parents have taught you, so please let them read this if it's different that what they have said to you.

I think it's really OK with God for us to dress fashionably, wear makeup, and try fun hairstyles. Most of the teenage girls I know aren't trying to be rebellious with their clothes or fashion, they just want to have fun and be cool.

In my house we have a few fashion guidelines: no shoulders or tummy showing in public. Too short or too low is also out. Nothing dark or sinister. Inside those boundaries, my daughter has permission to dress as hip or silly as she wants, and she does! She and her girlfriends have the best time putting things together.

God wired us to long for beautiful. He would not wire us for beautiful and then require us to pursue plain. So dress with integrity, but have as much fun as possible!

Angela Thomas is crazy about her four teenage and preteen kids. She is a great carpool driver, baseball watcher, and flat-iron stylist. When the kids can't think of anything else for her to do, she writes books for women and speaks at events around the country. www.angelathomas.com

REBEL WITH

Krystal Meyers

A CAUSE

by Sandy Smith

On the cover of her first CD, Krystal Meyers wears thick, metal chains around her neck, and heavy eye shadow darkens her face. A guitar is slung low over a hip, and chunky, leather bracelets grace both wrists. With a song like "Anticonformity" on the CD, it would be easy to label her as a modern rocker-chick who preaches rebellion.

And that label wouldn't be far off base. OK, so before you start thinking, *If my mom sees this article she'll wig out,* let's set the insurgent notion straight:

"Anticonformity means becoming the person God wants you to be and refusing to become the person that the world wants you to be," says Krystal.

> "Anticonformity means becoming the person God wants you to be and refusing to become the person that the world wants you to be," says Krystal.

It's pretty black and white; but that's Krystal, who got her start after a camp talent show led to a record deal. Now with her self-titled CD out, she's living the dream of any music-appreciating teenager.

At 16, she's traveled the country, rocking onstage and virtually living in the back of a van. During one stretch, she was away from home for more than six weeks solid, though her father Rick dropped into the tour from time to time.

Talk about a typical teen dream/ parental nightmare! But not for the Meyers family.

"I've been out there, and I see the people who are around her," says Rick. "I've heard her get into conversations with her band, and I know that she'd have a hard time getting into trouble with those guys around."

So how does one raise a grounded teenager who can be in the world aiming to make a difference but steadfastly refusing to be of the world? Krystal attributes that to her parents.

"They weren't raised in Christian homes, so when I'd come home emotionally distraught because all of my friends were doing stuff I knew I wasn't supposed to be doing, they were able to talk with me. [When they were teens, they'd gone with the flow of things and knew the consequences of that.] It was a great encouragement to keep saying no to the things I shouldn't be doing."

Being up front about their own failures "just seemed to make sense," Rick says. "We never wanted to lie or cover up anything. So we would tell Krystal, 'These are the signs that someone is dealing drugs or sneaking this or that.' She was able to confront her friends when they'd get there."

Just as her own parents were truthful about who they used to be, Krystal is frank with her friends and classmates about who she is and what she does and doesn't do.

"I figured out that a really safe thing

to do when you're first meeting new people [is to] be up front: 'I don't party. I don't do drugs. I'm going to be a virgin until I marry.' That leaves it open, if they're not down with that. It would be harder to say no if you worry about losing them," Krytal says.

The result has been people know what Krystal stands for.

"Instead of them shunning me and calling me 'Miss Goody Goody,' I had a ministry with them. They would come to me for advice, asking, 'What does the Bible say?' "

That philosophy has helped Krystal to remain friends with non-Christians, and it's helping her navigate the music industry.

"My parents taught me to have discernment. There's a very fine line there. I learned that I could be good friends in school, but when they'd go out and party, I didn't need to be there."

"You can say that Krystal's music is the world's music," Rick says. "She's trying to reach outside the church's walls. She'd say she's ministering to the world more than to the church. That seems to be her heart. She's always been a little missionary from the get-go. When she was 5, she'd go up to people and say, 'Do you know Jesus?' And she always liked her music loud."

And apparently, so do her fans. As a young woman in a male-dominated genre of Christian rock, Krystal's style surprises people.

"I've had people come up and say, 'I didn't think your show was going to be as rockin' as it was.' We just turn it up. We go all out and try to make it rock as hard as possible. We just can't be the little pop-punk girl opening the show for these bands. We've got to be up to par and rock-and-roll."

By doing so, Krystal hopes to start something of an anticonformity revolution. She's got a Web site— *www.anticonformity.net*—where teens can go to discuss their struggles to live a solid Christian life and find a community of those who also stand out a little bit.

"I have many a time when I've somehow stood out," writes a girl. "I listen to different music, dress different. Hey, I'm me! My interests are different from my friends. I love song/poetry writing while my friends are into 'This guy did this, this guy did that, did you hear…?' "

"I think it's cool that you're OK with who you are. We're all different. God just designed us that way," another responds.

Or, they can share typical angst. "I'd

be a punk, but my parents won't let me."

And of course, she meets her fans during concert tours. That's where they pour their hearts out.

"It's so cool. They're the exact same age as me. One girl in Chicago came up to me and was saying how my "Anticonformity" song touched her

and was encouragement to keep going against the flow in a public high school. 'I'm the only Christian among my friends. It was beginning to wear on me. Your song has become my life's anthem.' "

"It's very encouraging to keep doing what I do," the unconformed Krystal says. ✿

"I figured out that a really safe thing to do when you're first meeting new people (is to) be up front: 'I don't party. I don't do drugs. I'm going to be a virgin until I marry.' That leaves it open, if they're not down with that."

Spot the Beauty Myths
Quiz

Do you feel bombarded with messages about beauty? Take a look at your fashion magazines. What do they say to you about clothes, makeup, hairstyles, and your physical appearance?

Listed below are some lies about beauty. Read each one and answer from this point of view: Even though it may be silly to believe it, how much do I struggle with what this says? Be honest. Use the scale below to rate your answers.

    1 = I never believe this.
    2 = I believe this once in a while.
    3 = I believe this maybe half the time.
    4 = I believe this a lot.

1. Guys would rather date a cute girl than one with a good personality.
2. Having plastic surgery would make me like my body more.
3. I am prettier when I wear makeup.
4. Thinner girls are more attractive than bigger girls.
5. When I wear trendy clothes, I am more attractive.
6. Guys like it more when you show some skin.
7. Being beautiful will take you farther in life than if you aren't.
8. Cute girls will get more attention than average girls.
9. You have to do whatever it takes to look good.
10. If I could just change my appearance, I would be happier.
11. Pretty girls have higher self-esteem.
12. I don't feel good about myself when I look different from my friends.

Scoring: Add your scores to see the results of your Beauty Myths Test.

Beauty Boss

12–24: You passed with flying colors! You are able to withstand the pressure to believe these lies about beauty. Keep it up!

Cultural Cutie

25–36: You keep a thick skin, but lies do have a way of getting to you. It's OK to be critical of media messages. They don't always have your best interests in mind.

Doubting Deb

37–48: Maybe you know the truth in your head, but it hasn't yet made its way to your heart. God's truth the real thing? Choose to believe what He says, and your heart will follow.

Who are you to tell me
that I'm less than what I should be?
Who are you? Who are you?

—from "Mirror" by BarlowGirl

My World
7 days

Things to do this week to become the person God wants you to be.

1 bag the mags!
Take a break this week from looking at pop teen magazines. Don't forget to recycle.

2 real reflection
Cover your mirror for one day. Reflect on how God sees you.

3 warm fuzzies
Affirm someone every day this week for a non-physical attribute or characteristic.

4 the right stuff
Look for role models who dress modestly.

5 true to form
Evaluate what you wear this week by asking, "Is what I'm wearing honoring to God?"

6 prayer time
Pray for a friend who might have an eating disorder or an unhealthy view of herself.

7 work it on out
Exercise at least three times this week. Don't forget to warm up before your activity and take time to cool down at the end of your workout.

In My Own Words

The thing I struggle with about my
appearance is

The thing I like the most about the way
God made me is

The lie I have bought into the most is

innergirl
Time to Dance!

You are a
daughter
of the King!
And He is
wild about
you! That's
something
to celebrate!

Loving the Real Me

An Interview with Marcie Fairchild

Marcie Fairchild, a 20-year-old college student, is in love with God, life, and her authentic self. And she wants YOU to be wild about yourself too!

Marcie, describe the pressures you felt in high school.

God blessed me with some amazing gifts—intelligence, leadership, and a love for music. But during my freshman year of high school, these gifts became expectations. Unfortunately, I'm not talking about God's expectations for me to appreciate and share my gifts; I'm talking about the expectations of my parents, teachers, friends, and myself. In order not to disappoint anyone, I believed I had to excel at everything. I was determined to paint the picture of the perfect girl I thought I had to be. Soon, my involvement in every activity under the sun became the definition of who I was. I was so proud of everything that I had done and also of everything that I hadn't done (drinking, breaking curfew, premarital sex, etc.). But I still believed "I wasn't good enough," and that I never would be.

How did you deal with the pressure?

I pushed people away from what was really going on in my life. Though I was a Christian and extremely involved at church, I put God in a little section of my life—one that didn't involve my degenerating self-image. I became extremely depressed under my bubbly façade and resorted to cutting myself. I went to bed at night hoping not to wake up in the morning.

What was your turning point?

I was blessed with one person I could confide in who encouraged me to seek counseling. Counseling got me past suicidal thoughts, but it didn't put my life back together. It took a lot of time, but through a series of friends who lived God's love, I started to see how His love could really transform me. I now realize that I'm powerless and weak in the flesh, but complete and beautiful in Christ. This knowledge works every day on healing the brokenness that dominated my life for so long.

How did your life change after Christ rescued you from these pressures?

Things became less about me. I stopped "letting" God be a piece of my life; I let Him BE my life and saw myself as a piece of His plan. I'm able to enjoy my life and gifts, using them to serve Christ and not myself. After pretending to be someone else for so long, I'm now able to love myself for who I am. I get to be wild about me!

What would you say to girls who are going through the exact same thing?
Don't suffer in silence, and don't be afraid to get help. Find a Christian friend, parent, or mentor you can confide in.

Why is it so crucial for girls to see themselves through God's eyes?

When we neglect to see ourselves through God's eyes, and instead, look at ourselves through the eyes of the world, we easily fall into the routine of comparing ourselves to others and their ideals. Society makes us feel like we have to fit a certain mold, be a certain weight, land at the top of the class, and have a date every Friday night in order to be of worth. That simply isn't true! Through God's loving eyes, we can see that we are beautiful to Him, and He makes us complete. We are daughters of the King! And He truly is wild about each of us! That's really something to celebrate! ✽

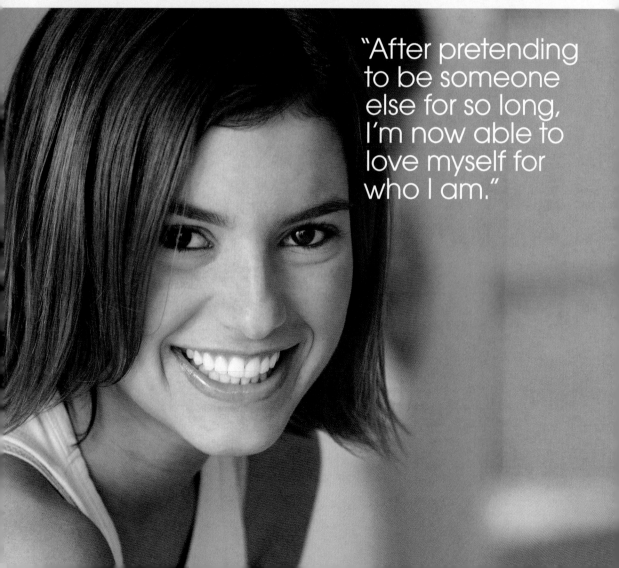

"After pretending to be someone else for so long, I'm now able to love myself for who I am."

Quiz Mall Maze

Ready for a challenge? Shopping can be like braving a minefield—everywhere you look there are messages trying to tell you to look a certain way or buy a certain thing in order to be happy. Using the skills you've learned, see how well you fare as you journey through this virtual mall. Circle the responses that mirror you.

1. You decide to try on a pair of jeans. What does that dressing room mirror tell you?
   a) "Those jeans make you look fat!"
   b) "Looking good, girl!"
   c) "They look OK, but you need to show some skin."

2. Your friend decides to get the top of her ear pierced and wants you to join her. Your parents would kill you. You:
   a) Go ahead. You can style your hair to cover it.
   b) Tell her you don't want to.
   c) Tell her the truth.

3. At the coffee shop you run into some girls from school who want you (but not your friend) to hang out. You:
   a) Tell them "no thanks."
   b) Find out where to meet up with them later—and don't tell your friend.
   c) Make a joke about your friend's ear, and when she gets mad at you, use that as a good excuse to ditch her.

4. Your friend suggests going to the lingerie store. She eyes your choice of underwear and calls you a grandma. How do you respond?
   a) Say, "I actually like my parts covered, thank you very much."
   b) Take a look at what you picked and feel stupid.
   c) Pick something more in-between.

5. You run into a cute guy from school. What's your response?
   a) You just smile and act yourself.
   b) You groan and think, My hair looks awful!
   c) You tell yourself, He won't even notice me.

6. You're at a cosmetics counter. Which of the following is what God's Word tells you?
   a) "If you wear this perfume you'll feel beautiful."
   b) "If you use this mascara, your eyes will look more beautiful."
   c) "If you believe what I say, you'll wear a crown of beauty."

Did you exit the mall with your self-esteem intact? Tally your score using this key.

	A	B	C			A	B	C
1.	1	3	2		4.	3	1	2
2.	1	2	3		5.	3	2	1
3.	3	2	1		6.	1	1	3

6-9 points: Do you have trouble believing what God says about you? Are you struggling with peer pressure, trying to fit in, or wanting approval from others? While all girls have these worries, you may need extra help learning to hear and believe God's Word above what the world says about you. Talk to your Bible study leader or a trusted adult about this quiz and your feelings.

10-14 points: You are learning to accept the truth that God is truly wild about you. You probably still have some trouble making the right choices when it comes to yielding to the overwhelming pressure to fit in. Keep studying what you've learned. Remember, God says you are gorgeous, believe it!

15-18 points: Way to go, girl! Whether you started this Bible study with a strong sense of self-assurance or changed the way you see yourself, it's clear that you know what God says about you. Continue to let those truths sink in!

VIEW

What's the secret of real beauty?

shining through

"If you're comfortable with who you are on the inside, it shows on the outside."
—Libby, 16

cool to the core

"The perfect girl is faithful and hopeful. She knows herself. She knows who she is. She secure in her core so she's not easily pressured by her friends."
—Brit, 17

get with him

"The secret of real beauty is a close relationship with God, and you cannot know Him unless you spend time with Him." —Alisa, 17

lovin' the real deal

"If you can't be happy with yourself, you won't ever be happy looking some other way."
—Meredith, 19

✳ instant message

There is no one on earth like you. God made you special, a unique beauty. He celebrates the real you and wants you to celebrate, too. Dance!

drop-dead gorgeous

"I feel prettiest on vacation. I'll go to Florida, and my hair's a mess, and I'm coming out of the ocean, and I feel beautiful. I don't feel the pressure to look any certain way. I can look drop-dead ugly and I can feel drop-dead gorgeous."
—Mandy, 15

innergirl

[Ask Angela]

starting over

Q I've already done some really dumb things that I feel awful about. How can I start over and stick to it this time?

A I love your honesty. Most of us don't get through life without a few dumb choices. But our God is so amazing that He runs to get us the moment we want to start over. And then He works in our favor to help us make better choices next time. Here's what to do:

1. Ask God for forgiveness and tell Him you want to start over. You may be suffering the consequences of things you have already done, so ask Him to give you grace to walk through those consequences with right thinking and integrity, even though it may be tough. Take each lesson to heart and decide what you have learned from the past.

2. Receive God's forgiveness. It's free for the asking, so thank Him for how great He is to give you forgiveness yet again.

3. Tell a couple of godly friends that you are starting over with God and ask them to walk beside you. Ask them to help you avoid new temptation and tell them you want them to ask you hard questions weekly or even daily if that would help in the beginning.

4. Hold your head up. God is not mad at you. More than anything, He wants your return and your devotion. So run with with everything you have back into His arms.

> Hold your head up. God is not mad at you. More than anything, He wants your return and your devotion. So run with everything you have back into His arms.

running strong?

Q I want to be a strong Christian, but most of my friends just come to church and don't really try to walk every day. I get distracted because I want to hang out with them, but I want to do the right thing too. Help!

A Wow. You have great insight. Friends don't have to be bad to keep you from growing in your relationship with God. You can have good friends who just aren't interested in spiritual things and who distract you.

Do you remember running in P.E. class? When you run, you pace yourself according to who is beside you. Some girls might run together up front and a pack of girls might hang together in the back, taking their time. It sounds like you are pacing with some slow runners.

Look around your school or youth group and find some girls who are excited about their relationship with God. Make an effort to spend time with them. When I spend time with a friend who is running fast toward God, she always makes me want to pick up my pace. It's fun to be beside her and grow toward God together.

Angela Thomas is crazy about her four teenage and preteen kids. She is a great carpool driver, baseball watcher, and flat-iron stylist. When the kids can't think of anything else for her to do, she writes books for women and speaks at events around the country. www.angelathomas.com

The Ring of Truth

by Kristi Cherry

"I didn't need anything or anyone else to say that I was worth something. God's approval and love were all I needed to be complete!"

NOTHING compares to my wedding day. As Dad placed my hand on Joseph's arm, it felt so right. I was his, and he was mine. In that moment, I felt incredibly close to God.

What did feeling close to God have to do with my wedding day? Everything! You see, my relationship with Joseph hadn't always been marriage-bound; the journey to the altar was long and bumpy. When we first began dating, I was always involved in something at school or church. Although I didn't know it at the time, my activities and endeavors were my way of searching for self-worth, something that would tell me, "Kristi, you're good enough; you're somebody."

Joseph began to give me some of the things I was searching to find. He affirmed me, respected me, and shared my desire to have a pure relationship. He even wrote me sweet notes. Wow! [Cue the dreamy music.] This is every girl's dream, right? But something wasn't right. [Stop the music.] I wasn't satisfied. Since I couldn't pinpoint why I wasn't happy, my relationship with Joseph fizzled out.

After college—when I didn't have classes and activities and friends taking up my time—I began to notice how empty my soul really was. It was then that I cried out to God. And there He was, stretching out His loving arms. Through a series of events and people, God showed me that He's the only One who can fulfill the longings in my soul. I read in His Word that I can have joy in Him, even when all else around me fails:

"Though the fig tree does not bud and there is no fruit on the vines, though the olive crop fails and the fields produce no food, though there are no sheep in the pen and no cattle in the stalls, yet I will triumph in the LORD; I will rejoice in the God of my salvation!" (Hab. 3:17-18).

And God did satisfy me. I didn't need anyone else to say I was worth something. His approval and love were all I needed to be complete! I drew closer to the Lord through studying the Bible and just giving all of myself to Him.

God was working on Joseph's heart at the same time, teaching him that he needed to be in love with God more than he was in love with me. As I grew closer to Christ, I saw Joseph doing the same. God pulled us back to each other. As we grew closer, our focus was on God. We both were complete in God; we weren't trying to fulfill each other or be fulfilled by each other. This made our relationship so much stronger.

Joseph asked me to marry him on a high hill overlooking the city lights. [Cue the dreamy music again.] He was down on one knee, with my hands in his, saying a bunch of romantic stuff that is all a blur to me now. I do remember that he remarked about how God had brought us to that place and how He would continue to be with us in our future life as husband and wife. I was shaking and trying to take it all in, but I managed to say, "YES!"

When you're filled by God and complete in Him, every other good thing is just a blessing! Today, I still rest in the same God and the complete joy He alone gives me. Being married to Joseph is just icing on the cake!❋

Dancing to the Truth

You've learned a lot in *six weeks*. Check it out—and celebrate!

1 I am not invisible! I was made to be seen and known and loved deeply. It's OK to want what I was made for.

I will celebrate by_____

2 God is wild about me! He made me special, thinks I'm gorgeous, and loves me just the way I am.

I will celebrate by_____

3 The part of me that aches to be filled is my soul, and my soul was made for God! His love makes me whole.

I will celebrate by_____

4 Neither a mirror nor a person has the right to tell me that I'm less than what I should be. I am complete in Christ!

I will celebrate by_____

5 My body is a gift from God. He created it the way He did for a reason.

I will celebrate by_____

6 The lies that I've been believing will only be silenced by listening to God's voice and what He says about me!

I will celebrate by_____

7 God's love, grace, and mercy are greater than my mistakes, doubts, and fears.

I will celebrate by_____

8 I cannot fall past God's love. I cannot outrun God's love. I cannot reach the end of God's love.

I will celebrate by_____

9 A good guy can be wonderful, but he can never be enough, and he can never make me whole. Only God can do that.

I will celebrate by_____

My Personal Beauty Philosophy

Write your own personal beauty philosophy. Here's what one girl wrote:

> My personal beauty philsophy is to discover my purpose in life and to always be true to myself and others! I will learn from my mistakes, continue dreaming, and do everything I can to make those dreams come true. I will balance a healthy life of school, church, family, and fun! I will learn to love myself and see myself through God's eyes. And I will smile first—and frown only when absolutely unavoidable!
> —B.J.

Now, it's your turn! Make your beauty philsophy as unique as you are.

My personal beauty philosophy is _____

_____

_____

_____

_____

_____

_____

_____

_____

_____

_____

"You are the noblest
of God's creations.
His intent is that your
life be gloriously
beautiful regardless
of your circumstances.
As you are grateful
and obedient, you can
become all that God
intends you to be."
—Richard G. Scott

MY WAY

The way I will celebrate my beautiful
body is

My absolute best physical feature is

because

I love the way my

EMOTIONAL CELEBRATION

"The best and most beautiful things in the world cannot be seen, nor touched but are felt in the heart." —Helen Keller

MY WAY

My way to celebrate my beautiful
emotions is

I love it when I can

I love the way I can use my emotions to
help others feel

innergirl

"Before one can walk as Christ walked and talk as He talked, she must first begin to think as Christ thought."
—A.A. Allen

MY WAY

My way to celebrate my beautiful
mind is

I love it when I push myself to think
about

I love the way I can use my brain to

"Since love grows within you, so beauty grows. For love is the beauty of the soul."
—Saint Augustine

MY WAY

My way to celebrate my beautiful
soul is

When I think about my soul I

The way I celebrate my spiritual
soul is

Model Citizens

Back Row:
**Melva and
Mae**
Middle Row:
**Irish, Nhi,
and Ella**
Front Row:
**Arlyn and
Cheryl**

**NAME: Nhi Duong
(pronounced "nee")
HOMETOWN: Fort Smith, Arkansas**

MODEL ACTION: Two-week mission trip to the Philippines

MOTIVATION: A Christian guy I know went to Kenya and came home changed. I asked God to use me one day, too. When I heard about this trip, I knew God wanted me to go.

SIGNIFICANT EXPERIENCE: I talked to a Filipino pastor about his daughter, Jac Jac. He and his wife adopted Jac Jac when she was only two months old after her mother died. That was amazing to me because pastors in the Philippines endure lots of hardship, poverty, and sickness.

TAKE AWAY: No matter what, God looks out for the tiniest child. If He takes care of the birds, He will take care of me, too. I also learned that people who have little appreciate more what God gives them.

FUTURE PLANS: My family migrated here from Vietnam when I was young. I want to get my education as a physical therapist and return to Vietnam as a missionary to my own people.

FAVORITE QUOTE: "However appealing the whole universe is, it is still worth less than the heart of Jesus."
—György Orbán

Nicole Spedick (left) with her cousin, **Allie Shilling**

**NAME: Nicole Spedick
HOMETOWN: Bend, Oregon**

MODEL ACTION: Intern at International Justice Mission, a human rights agency that rescues victims of violence, sexual exploitation, slavery, and oppression

(For more information on IJM, visit *www.ijm.org*.)

Allison and Angela Banks

MOTIVATION: A friend told me about IJM. I looked up the Web site and I watched the rescue of women and girls out of brothels in Thailand. It was all I could do to whisper, "I want to be a part of this, Lord!"

SIGNIFICANT EXPERIENCE: A worker from Thailand came to visit and shared stories and pictures of the girls she had been working to rescue from forced prostitution. The pictures broke my heart; I realized that even the mundane tasks I had done made a difference.

TAKE AWAY: There is nothing else that I want to do but live to serve others. No other pursuit is as satisfying or fulfilling—or as challenging!

FAVORITE QUOTE: "I am only one; but still I am one. I cannot do everything, but still I can do something; I will not refuse to do something I can do."
— Edward Hale

NAME: Allison and Angela Banks
HOMETOWN: Wichita Falls, Texas

MODEL ACTION: Twice-weekly Bible study/accountability group on their high school campus

MOTIVATION: On a band trip, a bunch of us were talking on the bus. The conversation turned to religion, and we decided it would be cool to get together to talk about it more.

SIGNIFICANT EXPERIENCE: It's been cool to see kids of different beliefs come together—including Methodist, Baptist, and Catholic. We all have different opinions, but nobody ever gets mad. We all go back to the Bible as our standard and our source.

TAKE AWAY: (Angela) It's important to meet people where they are. Not everyone comes from a church background. You have to learn how to accept where they are in their faith journey. (Allison) I've learned how much others depend on me. I'll be in the hallway and someone will say, "We're having Bible study today, aren't we?" That's when I realized people are counting on me.

FAVORITE QUOTE: "Be a missionary on campus disguised as a student."
—Bill Banks (their dad!)

Do Life Better!

Physical

1. Go walking or jogging with a friend.
2. Color your world: eat an apple, orange, or banana every day!
3. Use canned vegetables as handweights to lift while you're doing homework or watching TV.

Your Give-away Coupon

This coupon good for

(insert your special physical-based act of service)

compliments of

Do Life Better!

Emotional

1. Refuse to listen to sad, melancholy music with depressing lyrics.
2. Write an encouraging note to one of your teachers.
3. Give five compliments every day.

Your Give-away Coupon

This coupon good for

(insert your special emotion-based act of service)

because I love you, compliments of

Do Life Better!

Mental

CLIP AND SAVE

1. Memorize one Scripture passage every week.
2. Starve negative thoughts by stopping them as they pop in your head.
3. Research possible careers related to your favorite subject in school.

Your Give-away Coupon

(insert name)

I think you're gorgeous and God does too.

Your Friend,

Do Life Better!

Spiritual

1. Write out or sing your prayers to God.
2. Read a psalm every morning. Read a chapter of Proverbs every night.
3. When you walk into school each day, pray for God to use you.

Your Give-away Coupon

I'm praying for you today

_____
(insert name)

because I care about you. Your friend,

_____

In My Own Words

The most important thing I've learned from "Wild About You" is

The thing that I most want to work on is

The greatest thing about knowing that God thinks I'm gorgeous is

because

If I could sit down and talk face-to-face with Jesus about how I feel about myself now, I would tell Him